Judith Weiblen

Determining Cycle Times for Packing in Distribution Centres

WISSENSCHAFTLICHE BERICHTE

Institut für Fördertechnik und Logistiksysteme
am Karlsruher Institut für Technologie (KIT)

BAND 82

Determining Cycle Times for Packing in Distribution Centres

by
Judith Weiblen

Dissertation, Karlsruher Institut für Technologie (KIT)
Fakultät für Maschienenbau, 2014
Referenten:　Prof. Dr.-Ing. Kai Furmans
　　　　　　　Ass.-Prof. PhD Daniel Hellström

Impressum

Karlsruher Institut für Technologie (KIT)
KIT Scientific Publishing
Straße am Forum 2
D-76131 Karlsruhe

KIT Scientific Publishing is a registered trademark of Karlsruhe Institute of Technology. Reprint using the book cover is not allowed.

www.ksp.kit.edu

　This document – excluding the cover – is licensed under the
　　　　　　　Creative Commons Attribution-Share Alike 3.0 DE License
(CC BY-SA 3.0 DE): http://creativecommons.org/licenses/by-sa/3.0/de/

　The cover page is licensed under the Creative Commons
　　　　　　　Attribution-No Derivatives 3.0 DE License (CC BY-ND 3.0 DE):
http://creativecommons.org/licenses/by-nd/3.0/de/

Print on Demand 2014

ISSN 0171-2772
ISBN 978-3-7315-0202-9
DOI: 10.5445/KSP/1000040086

Determining Cycle Times for Packing in Distribution Centres

Zur Erlangung des akademischen Grades eines

Doktors der Ingenieurwissenschaften

der Fakultät für Maschinenbau
des Karlsruher Instituts für Technologie (KIT)
genehmigte

Dissertation

von

Dipl.-Wi.-Ing. Judith Weiblen

aus Mannheim

Tag der mündlichen Prüfung: 17. März 2014
Hauptreferent: Prof. Dr.-Ing. Kai Furmans
Korreferent: Ass.-Prof. PhD Daniel Hellström

Vorwort

Die vorliegende Arbeit entstand während meiner Tätigkeit als wissenschaftliche Mitarbeiterin am Institut für Fördertechnik und Logistiksysteme des Karlsruher Instituts für Technologie (KIT). Durch die hierbei erworbenen Kenntnisse, die durch die mannigfaltige Ausrichtung dieser Tätigkeit in den Gebieten Forschung, Industrieprojekte und Lehre geprägt sind, wurde die Erstellung der Arbeit erst ermöglicht.

Für diese Arbeit richtungsweisend war vor allem das Verbundforschungsprojekt Versandverpacken, bei dem wir durch die beachtliche Unterstützung zahlreicher Unternehmen einen Eindruck über die Vielfältigkeit von Verpackungstätigkeiten gewinnen sowie technische und betriebswirtschaftliche Daten in diesem Bereich erheben konnten.

Dieses Vorwort möchte ich nutzen, um all denen zu danken, die zum Gelingen der vorliegenden Dissertationsschrift beigetragen haben.

Herrn Prof. Dr.-Ing. Kai Furmans, Leiter des Instituts für Fördertechnik und Logistiksysteme, gilt mein besonderer Dank für die Anwerbung, Übernahme des Hauptreferats sowie für die Unterstützung meiner Tätigkeit als wissenschaftliche Mitarbeiterin.

Herrn Ass.-Prof. PhD Daniel Hellström danke ich für die Übernahme des Korreferats, sowie die Möglichkeit zum Forschungsaufenthalt an der Universität Lund und die interessanten Diskussionen.

Frau Prof. Dr.-Ing. Gisela Lanza danke ich vielmals für die Übernahme des Prüfungsvorsitzes.

Der dreimonatige Forschungsaufenthalt an der Universität Lund in Schweden wurde vom Karlsruher House of Young Scientists (KHYS) gefördert und damit erst möglich, vielen Dank. Diese Zeit gab mir Gelegenheit mich grundlegend in die Thematik einzuarbeiten und die Basis der Dissertationsschrift zu legen. Vielen Dank auch an die Kollegen der Packaging Logistics Abteilung in Lund für die angenehme Zeit und den kollegialen Rahmen.

Natürlich möchte ich mich auch bei allen aktiven und ehemaligen Kollegen des Instituts für Fördertechnik und Logisitksysteme bedanken. Die angenehme Arbeitsatmosphäre war ein ausschlaggebender Grund für mich die Herausforderungen als wissenschaftliche Mitarbeiterin anzunehmen. Die gemeinsamen Unternehmungen werden mir allein schon wegen der zahlreichen Fotos in meinen Alben in guter Erinnerung bleiben.

Mein besonderer Dank gilt auch meinen drei Korrekturlesern, für die investierte Zeit sowie besonders auch für die Anregungen und Diskussionen.

Mein tiefster, persönlicher Dank gilt meiner Familie, insbesondere meinen Eltern und meinem Bruder, die mich auf meinem Weg unterstützten und diesen überhaupt erst ermöglicht haben. Mein größter Dank gilt meinem Freund für den langjährigen gemeinsamen Lebensweg, die dabei entgegengebrachte Liebe und vor allem die Unterstützung und das Verständnis in Bezug auf das Entstehen dieser Arbeit.

Karlsruhe, März 2014   Judith Weiblen

Kurzfassung

Judith Weiblen

Bestimmung von Spielzeiten für das Versandverpacken in Distributionszentren

Das Konsolidieren und Verpacken ist der zweitwichtigste Prozess in Distributionszentren sowohl in Bezug auf Kosten als auch auf die benötigte Arbeitszeit. In dieser Arbeit werden allgemeine Spielzeitformeln zur Berechnung von zeitlichen Aufwänden für das Versandverpacken in Distributionszentren hergeleitet. Mit Hilfe dieser Formeln kann bei der Planung eines neuen Distributionszentrums die benötigte Anzahl an Packplätzen bestimmt werden. Die Vorgehensweise wurde von Grund auf neu entwickelt, da bisher noch keine Ansätze für das Versandverpacken existieren.

Basierend auf einer Literaturrecherche wird ein allgemeiner Versandverpackungsprozess identifiziert, dessen Materialfluss mit Hilfe von Prozessketten dargestellt wird. Darüber hinaus werden auch der Informationsfluss sowie die Organisation des Verpackprozesses charakterisiert. Um alle zeitrelevanten Parameter übersichtlich abzubilden, wird für jeden der identifizierten Teilprozesse eine morphologische Box erstellt. Im folgenden Schritt werden, mit Hilfe von Varianzanalysen (ANOVA), signifikante Parameter identifiziert. Die signifikantesten Parameter werden anschließend in einer gemeinsamen morphologischen Box zusammengefasst, die den gesamten Packprozess umfasst. Diese kann einerseits zur Priorisierung von Verbesserungsmaßnahmen von existierenden Packplätzen verwendet werden, andererseits werden diese Parameter bei der Ableitung der Spielzeit besonders berücksichtigt. Die Spielzeiten werden in Anlehnung an die bereits existierenden allgemeinen Spielzeiten des Kommissionierprozesses in Distributionszentren erstellt. Die Größe einer Einheit, einer der signifikantesten

Parameter in der Analyse, wird verwendet, um standardisierte Aufgaben im Versandverpacken, die unterschiedlichen Aufwand erfordern, zu definieren. Mit Hilfe dieser Aufgaben können Werte der allgemeinen Formeln präzisiert und darüber hinaus vorhandene Verpackungsbereiche im Rahmen eines Benchmarks verglichen werden. Zur Validierung werden die Spielzeitformeln mit Hilfe der beiden in der Praxis am häufigsten auftretenden Aufgaben ausgeprägt, verfeinert sowie mit Praxiswerten verglichen. Zusätzlich wird die Allgemeingültigkeit der Formeln in einer Fallstudie für eine ungewöhnliche Verpackungsaufgabe überprüft. Beide Vorgehensweisen bestätigen, dass die abgeleiteten allgemeinen Spielzeitformeln zur Berechnung von Bearbeitungszeiten für Verpackungsaufgaben in Distributionszentren eingesetzt werden können.

Abstract

Judith Weiblen
Determining cycle times for packing in distribution centres

This thesis determines general cycle time formulas which can be used to calculate the time needed for packing in distribution centres. These formulas help planners to calculate the number of packing workplaces required when setting up a new distribution centre. Surprisingly, considering that consolidation and packing represent the second most important process in terms of costs and working time in a distribution centre, no cycle time calculations for packing are available to date.

The thesis begins with a literature review and the definition of a standardised packing process which is illustrated using a process chain for the material flow. The information flow and the organisation of packing are also examined. For each identified sub-process, we create a morphological box in order to structure all the parameters influencing packing time. This then forms the basis for identifying of significant parameters with the help of analysis of variance (ANOVA). These significant parameters are summarised in one common morphological box for all the process steps. This can be used to prioritise measures as part of an improvement process to optimise existing packing workplaces. Additionally, it helps to set the focus when determining cycle times. Existing approaches to calculating general cycle times for another process in distribution centres, picking, are followed where possible. We use one of the most significant parameters, unit size, to differentiate the packing process according to the efforts needed for the task. This structure can be utilised in the future as a benchmark to compare existing packing processes. In this thesis, this structure is used to identify the two most common packing cases in distribution centres and to refine values for the calculation formulas applied to them. The results are compared with existing processes to enhance the credibility of the cycle time formulas. Moreover, we carried out a case study of an implemented, very specific packing task in order to validate the general applicability of the cycle times. The results of both approaches show that the general cycle time formulas derived here can be used to calculate the time required for packing in distribution centres.

Contents

Kurzfassung	iii
Abstract	v
List of Figures	xi
List of Tables	xiii

1 Introduction   1
    1.1 Problem Statement 3
    1.2 Organisation of the Thesis 4

2 Background   7
    2.1 Distribution Centres 7
       2.1.1 Function and Types 8
       2.1.2 Processes 9
    2.2 Packing 11
       2.2.1 Packing in General 12
       2.2.2 Packing in Distribution Centres 13
    2.3 Cycle Times 15
       2.3.1 Definition and Purpose 15
       2.3.2 Overview and Use Cases 16
       2.3.3 Picking 19

3 Related work   23
    3.1 Design for Manual Packaging 23
    3.2 Process Cost Model for Manual Packing Workplaces . . . 25
    3.3 Development of Optimised Operation Strategies for Sorting Systems 28

4 Defining the Packing Process — 33
- 4.1 Material Flow — 34
  - 4.1.1 Prepare Job — 36
  - 4.1.2 Prepare Packaging — 37
  - 4.1.3 Pack — 37
  - 4.1.4 Check — 38
  - 4.1.5 Protect — 39
  - 4.1.6 Insert Add-in — 40
  - 4.1.7 Secure — 40
  - 4.1.8 Mark — 42
  - 4.1.9 Provide — 43
- 4.2 Information Flow — 43
- 4.3 Organisation — 45
  - 4.3.1 Organisational Structure — 46
  - 4.3.2 Operational Structure — 47

5 Morphological Analysis — 51
- 5.1 Definition of the Problem — 52
- 5.2 Determination of Influencing Parameters — 53
  - 5.2.1 Prepare Job — 53
  - 5.2.2 Prepare Packaging — 57
  - 5.2.3 Pack — 60
  - 5.2.4 Check — 63
  - 5.2.5 Protect — 65
  - 5.2.6 Insert Add-in — 67
  - 5.2.7 Secure — 69
  - 5.2.8 Mark — 71
  - 5.2.9 Provide — 72
- 5.3 Analysis of the Morphological Boxes — 74
  - 5.3.1 Predetermined Motion Time Systems — 76
  - 5.3.2 Analysis of Variance — 78
  - 5.3.3 Results from Analysis of Variance — 82
- 5.4 Refining the Solution and Implications for Cycle Time — 93

6 Determining Cycle Times for Packing — 99
- 6.1 Cycle Time General Formula — 100
- 6.2 Travel Time — 103
- 6.3 Set-up Time — 106

	6.4	Base Time	107
	6.5	Item Time	108

7 Validation   111
    7.1   Derivation and Selection of Tasks for Validation 112
    7.2   Packing Articles in Packages or Small Load Carriers . . . 115
         7.2.1   Travel Time 115
         7.2.2   Set-up Time 116
         7.2.3   Base Time 117
         7.2.4   Item Time 120
         7.2.5   Proof of Concept 121
    7.3   Packing Packages or Small Load Carriers on Pallets . . . 125
         7.3.1   Travel Time 125
         7.3.2   Set-up Time 126
         7.3.3   Base Time 127
         7.3.4   Item Time 129
         7.3.5   Proof of Concept 130
    7.4   Case Study 133

8 Conclusion   139
    8.1   Summary 139
    8.2   Outlook 142

References   145

A Detailed Analysis of Set-up Times for P10   157

B Detailed Analysis of Set-up Times for P5   161

C Glossary of Notations   165
    C.1   Notations Chapter 3.3 165
    C.2   Notations Chapter 5.3 166
    C.3   Notations Chapter 6 and 7 167

List of Figures

1.1 A: Distribution of costs in distribution centres, n=17; B: Distribution of working time in distribution centres, n=19 (Data from Warehouse Excellence Study, 2013) 2
1.2 Structure of this thesis 4

2.1 Processes in distribution centres (following Wisser 2009, 10) 10
2.2 Different types of packaging 14

4.1 Sub-systems of the packing process (by analogy to Lolling 2003, 7) 34
4.2 Packing process steps of the material flow system 35
4.3 Distribution of checking methods, n=80 (Weiblen and Berbig 2011) 39
4.4 Precedence graph for the packing process 47

5.1 Working zones for different activities (following Bokranz and Landau 2006, 280) 59
5.2 Share of application and awareness for different motion time systems (Sautter et al. 1998, 47) 77

7.1 Packing tasks in distribution centres (Weiblen et al. 2012) 113
7.2 Incidence of tasks in distribution centres, n=212 (Weiblen and Berbig 2011) 114

List of Tables

5.1	Morphological box for 'prepare job'	54
5.2	Morphological box for 'prepare packaging'	58
5.3	Morphological box for 'pack'	60
5.4	Morphological box for 'check'	63
5.5	Morphological box for 'protect'	66
5.6	Morphological box for 'insert add-in'	68
5.7	Morphological box for 'secure'	69
5.8	Morphological box for 'mark'	72
5.9	Morphological box for 'provide'	73
5.10	Parameters with analysed specifications for 'prepare job'	83
5.11	2_{III}^{15-11} fractional factorial design for 'prepare job'	84
5.12	ANOVA table for 'prepare job'	85
5.13	ANOVA table for 'common parameters'	87
5.14	ANOVA table for 'prepare packaging'	87
5.15	ANOVA table for 'pack'	88
5.16	ANOVA table for 'check'	89
5.17	ANOVA table for 'protect'	90
5.18	ANOVA table for 'insert add-in'	91
5.19	ANOVA table for 'secure'	91
5.20	ANOVA table for 'mark'	92
5.21	ANOVA table for 'provide'	93
5.22	Resulting condensed morphological box for packing	98
6.1	Typical de-/acceleration and velocity values following Gudehus (1973, 58)	105
7.1	Typical values for set-up times for P10 using MTM	117
7.2	Typical times for packing single units following MTM-UAS	120
7.3	Typical values for set-up times for P5 using MTM	127

A.1	Detailed analysis of 'choosing job' (P10)	157
A.2	Detailed analysis of 'confirmation on start' (P10)	158
A.3	Detailed analysis of 'identification' (P10)	158
A.4	Detailed analysis of 'decision on packaging' (P10)	158
A.5	Detailed analysis of 'decision on protection material' (P10)	159
A.6	Detailed analysis of 'decision on securing method' (P10)	159
A.7	Detailed analysis of 'initialisation print' (P10)	159
A.8	Detailed analysis of 'marking' (P10)	160
B.1	Detailed analysis of 'choosing job' (P5)	161
B.2	Detailed analysis of 'confirmation on start' (P5)	162
B.3	Detailed analysis of 'identification' (P5)	162
B.4	Detailed analysis of 'decision on packaging' (P5)	163
B.5	Detailed analysis of 'decision on protection material' (P5)	163
B.6	Detailed analysis of 'decision on securing method' (P5)	163
B.7	Detailed analysis of 'initialisation print' (P5)	164
B.8	Detailed analysis of 'marking' (P5)	164

1 Introduction

Supply chains are faced with increasing globalisation and market volatility. According to Baker (2006, 207), this is particularly challenging for distribution centres because they represent key nodes in supply chains, accounting for approximately 17 percent of the total logistics costs (in 2008 according to Mayer 2009). This means that distribution centres have to demonstrate a high degree of flexibility, but be efficient at the same time.

Rouwenhorst et al. (2000, 515) explain that costs within a distribution centre are already determined to a large extent during the design phase. Especially costs linked to oversizing can be avoided during this phase. To avoid oversizing while planning, precise data are needed about the system throughput performance (Seemüller 2005, 84). Throughput is usually calculated using mean cycle times for a typical operating cycle of the system (Seemüller 2005, 2), where the throughput is the reciprocal of the cycle time (VDI 4480-2, 2).

Gudehus (1973, 9) states that cycle times existed for production systems in the 1970s, but that the dimensioning of picking systems, another process in distribution centres, was based on trial and error. He remarks that planning and optimising are only possible if general rules and calculations are available. Besides planning and optimising, cycle times are also helpful for manufacturers or operators when assessing systems (VDI 4480-2, 2, VDI 3978, 2, VDI 4418, 25).

Since the 1970s, there has been a lot of research done on the cycle times for different picking systems (for a summary cf. Lippolt 2003, Sarker and Babu 1995). However, picking is not the only process performed in a distribution centre. After picking, packing into different container sizes or unit loads has to be done to be able to ship and handle individual items more efficiently (Bowersox et al. 2010, 29). As a consequence, packing was

(Lange 1998, 112) and still is (cf. Figure 1.1; Bartholdi III and Hackman 2011, 23) one of the most important processes in terms of costs and working time in distribution centres. The share of time is even larger than the share of costs, as packing is hardly automated to ensure flexibility and is therefore very labour-intensive (Bartholdi III and Hackman 2011, 28, Jodin and ten Hompel 2006, 55, Wiese 1996, 17).

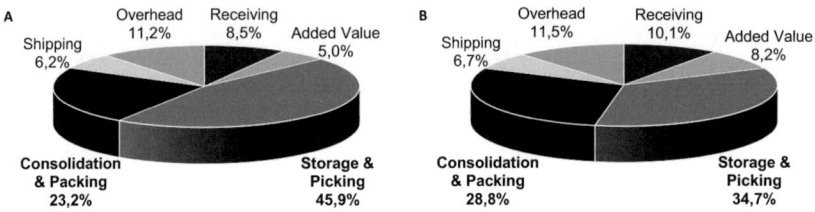

Figure 1.1: A: Distribution of costs in distribution centres, n=17; B: Distribution of working time in distribution centres, n=19 (Data from Warehouse Excellence Study, 2013)

In spite of its importance, Stock (2001, 132) considers packaging to be an under-researched area. One reason might be that, according to Lange (1998, 112) and Scherff (1987, 15), packing is very complex, especially regarding its requirements, methods and technology. Despite these challenges, when planning a packing system, it is necessary to decide which system should be chosen to achieve the best efficiency and how many workplaces will be necessary to meet the demands of the given packing task (Dzeik 2008, 19).

Another challenge is that packing affects the processes up- and downstream. Radtke (2000, 133) shows that packing has an effect on sorting and describes the packing system as a performance-limiting component for the sorting system. This is a further motivation for not simply sizing the packing system based on experience, but using scientifically-derived formulas and eventually combining them with those of other processes.

As previously mentioned, cycle times are commonly used for this purpose. However, there are no cycle times for packing workplaces at present and sizing is simply based on staff experience. As a result, many packing areas have workplaces which have proved to be unsuitable for the required amount of packages to be packed per day (cf. Weiblen and Breiner 2012, 201).

1.1 Problem Statement

In order to determine the required size of a packing area, the planner needs to answer the following question among others: How many packing workplaces are needed to handle the required throughput? A sufficient number is needed to accomplish this task, but too many workplaces would be a waste of investment, which is usually restricted or should be at a minimum.

To answer this question, the planner needs to know two facts. First, how many units need to be packed per day, which is usually given as part of the functional description (Rouwenhorst et al. 2000, 515). Second, how long it takes to pack one unit. In order to determine the time necessary for packing, we need to know which process steps are essential to complete the required shipping unit.

The next step is to calculate the time needed for each individual step. In order to do this, we also need to know which parameter influence the time needed. Once the influencing parameters are known, the planner can decide which packing method is appropriate (including technical specifications, equipment selection and determination of layout; cf. Rouwenhorst et al. 2000, 515).

If cycle time calculations existed for every method, the planner could also use these cycle times to calculate and compare methods. But, as already mentioned, there is a lack of research on packing operations in distribution centres and a proposal for how to calculate cycle times for packing does not even exist. At the same time, systematic planning and optimisation are only possible if the basic facts are known and therefore predictable, which yields common rules and calculation methods (Gudehus 1973, 9).

Therefore, this thesis aims to answer the question of how to calculate cycle times for packing scenarios in distribution centres. This serves as a starting point for further research. In order to achieve general validity, specific technical implementations or strategies are not examined in more detail.

To start with, the packing process is defined, described and structured, and important influencing parameters are identified, which have to be considered when calculating and specifying packing times. At the same time, these are also indicators of effective improvement measures.

Based on these results, we derive a general cycle time calculation method and validate it for its applicability and generality. This calculation method lays the foundation for calculating cycle times for packing, and can be applied to packing scenarios by specifying its components.

1.2 Organisation of the Thesis

The chapters in this thesis are structured as shown in Figure 1.2.

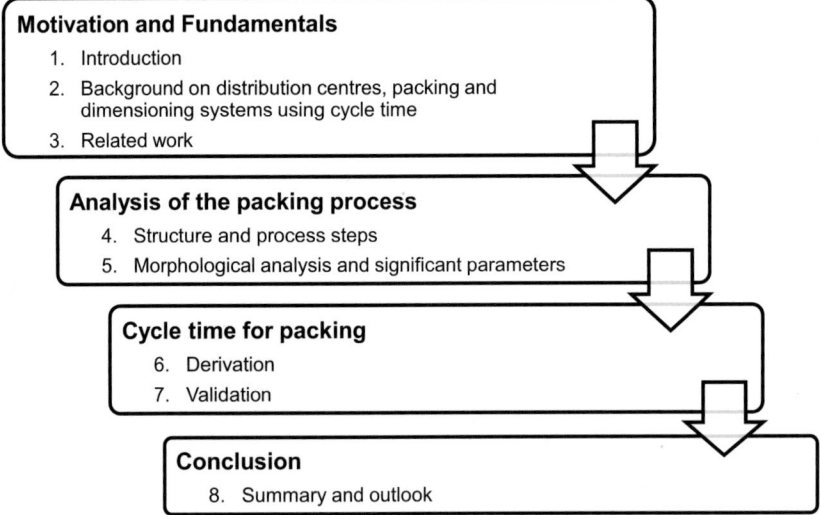

Figure 1.2: Structure of this thesis

First of all, Chapter 2 gives an overview of the processes performed in distribution centres, their interactions, as well as detailed information about packing. The second section of this chapter focuses on cycle times,

1.2 Organisation of the Thesis

especially in the distribution centre context. Together, this theoretical foundation serves as a reference point for deriving cycle times for packing in distribution centres.

Chapter 3 then discusses the work of several authors who have performed research in this area, and shows how their work is related to the research covered in this thesis. Important implications of their research are highlighted.

The next two chapters structure and analyse the packing process in detail. Chapter 4 structures the packing process in distribution centres regarding material flow, organisation and information flow, and considers the literature on packing. This is important to understand packing in distribution centres, and to be able to construct morphological boxes with parameters influencing the packing time in the following chapter.

Having defined the problem, we construct morphological boxes in Chapter 5. The boxes include time-relevant parameters and their specifications. Analysis of variance (ANOVA) is then applied to identify the most important influencing parameters. These parameters are summarised and taken into account when deriving the cycle time.

Based on these results, Chapter 6 starts by identifying the assumptions which have to be made in order to derive a general method for calculating cycle times. The cycle time calculation is derived and the single components of travel time, set-up time, base time, and item time are specified using detailed formulas.

In order to validate these formulas, in Chapter 7, the most significant parameter, unit size, is used to derive tasks which describe different packing scenarios which differ by the amount of effort required. The two most common tasks are looked at more closely to judge whether the derived method can be applied to these cases and if the calculated values are realistic. To finalise validation, a case study is also made of the cycle times of a specific scenario.

Finally, Chapter 8 summarises the results of this research and indicates the need for future research based on the insights acquired.

2 Background

The distribution process distributes goods in order to bridge differences in time and space between production and demand (DIN 30781-1, 2). It starts right after the production process, where the last step is to pack goods in order to make them transportable. The process ends, as soon as the consumer uses the package, usually by removing the good out of the package (Bleisch et al. 2011, 46).

Within this distribution network, from production to the customer, the good passes nodes, which are usually called distribution centres. There, the package might need to be repacked, sometimes together with different products, to be able to handle them efficiently (Bartholdi III and Hackman 2011, 23). In this chapter, we first focus on distribution centres, before having a closer look at the packing process within these centres. Further, we focus on cycle times: on their definition, where they are applied, and how they can be structured, with a focus on cycle times in distribution centres.

2.1 Distribution Centres

A distribution centre or distribution warehouse, according to Frazelle (2002, 226-227) and Martin (2009, 6-7), accumulates and consolidates products from various points of manufacturing for combined shipment to common customers. Thereby, the origin of the products might be within a single company or several companies. Pfohl (2010, 112) adds that, in these nodes of a logistic network, goods are stored temporarily or they are just routed to another destination. Accordingly, the movement may be typified by the following cases:

- Full pallets or cases in and out, or

- Full pallets or cases in and broken case quantities out (Frazelle 2002, 226-227; Bartholdi III and Hackman 2011, 23).

Representing an additional node, and thus another tier in the supply chain, distribution centres are often associated with additional costs (ten Hompel et al. 2007, 2, 13).

2.1.1 Function and Types

But why do distribution centres exist then? Summarizing Bartholdi III and Hackman (2011, 5-7), ten Hompel and Schmidt (2010, 3-5), Martin (2009, 6-7), Arnold et al. (2004, B7-7) and Govindaraj et al. (2000, 1099), we can identify the following reasons for having distribution centres:

- To better match supply with customer demand.
- To transfer homogeneous input streams to customer-specific output streams.
- To provide customer service.
- To handle returns.
- To consolidate products in order to reduce transportation costs.
- To optimise logistic performance.
- To assure production capability.
- To process goods.

Having a distribution centre means having an additional tier in the distribution process. According to Arnold et al. (2004, B7-7), this additional tier only pays off if the costs for one of the above reasons are lower than with shipping directly. As a consequence, optimising processes within distribution centres is a key lever to improve the overall supply chain efficiency.

Considering the different functions of a distribution centre mentioned above, different kinds of distribution centres are distinguished by several authors: Rouwenhorst et al. (2000, 518-519) differ between distribution and production warehouses. The function of a distribution warehouse is to store products and to fulfil external customer orders, typically composed of a large number of order lines. Whereas the function of a production warehouse is to store raw materials, work-in-progress and finished products, associated with a manufacturing and/or assembly process. Bartholdi III and Hackman (2011, 8-10) structure centres according to their goods and business model:

- Retail distribution centre
- Service parts distribution centre
- Catalogue fulfilment or e-commerce
- 3PL warehouse
- Perishables warehouse

Pfohl (2010, 112) distinguishes centres according to their purpose: storage, transshipment and distribution. Thereby, often storage centres are referred to as warehouses, the second ones as transshipment points or cross docks, and the last ones as distribution centres.

We will focus on distribution centres in this thesis but, as Pfohl (2010, 112) emphasises, there are hybrids in practice and borders cannot be clearly drawn. Hence, the models which will be developed in this thesis could be applied to other warehouses or packing processes like for example in transshipment points as well.

2.1.2 Processes

The variety in types results in different structures of distribution centres and therefore different process structures. Wisser (2009, 11-16), for example, distinguishes six processes within a distribution centre but comments that not every distribution centre needs to execute all of them. In the following, processes are distinguished and described according to Pfohl (2010, 117-120), ten Hompel and Schmidt (2010, 23-53), Wisser (2009, 12-16), Rouwenhorst et al. (2000, 516-517) and Magee et al. (1985, 153), and shown in Figure 2.1.

The process inside the distribution centre starts with arriving goods in the receiving area, which is at the same time one of the two links to

Figure 2.1: Processes in distribution centres (following Wisser 2009, 10)

the outside. Goods arrive by truck or internal transport and need to be unloaded. Identifying, checking, inspecting or even repacking might be necessary as well, before goods are provided for the following process.

The following process is usually the storing of goods. For this purpose, a suitable storage location is chosen (e.g. according to the size of the unit), the unit is transported to and registered on the specific storage location to be able to retrieve it later. Often, there are also different storage areas, such as one for reserve or unit stock and one forward area for easy retrieval by order-pickers.

The next step is the picking or retrieval of the goods. This usually takes place when there is customer demand and picking lists are generated according to optimisation criteria. The picking process includes travelling of a person or machine to the storage location, grasping of whole units or parts and transporting of goods, in order to provide them for the next process. It depends on the customer order and the organisation of the distribution centre whether this is the consolidation, packing, shipping or added value process.

One reason for having a consolidation or sorting area is that items of one order are stored in different areas, picked in parallel and it is necessary to group them for shipping. This is a very common reason, but there are also other reasons that make consolidation necessary. According to the purpose of the system, there are many possibilities for organising and implementing the process (for details cf. Jodin and ten Hompel 2006).

Sometimes, the next process of packing goods for one order into shipping containers or on unit loads is regarded as part of shipping. It is not necessarily only one packing step (Dzeik 2008, 33), but there might be several packing steps: e.g. goods have to be packed into a corrugated container, before several of these containers can be packed onto a pallet in order to handle them more efficiently (cf. Chapter 4). Packing in distribution centres is characterised by grouping a big variety of goods in different combinations. Therefore, a big variety of packing solutions can be found.

Finally, these units are transported to the shipping area, where they are loaded into trucks, trains or any other carriers, and secured for transportation. Also sorting, to separate destinations, and buffering units in the shipping area for a short time, in order to achieve full truck loads, might be necessary. The shipping process is the other process besides receiving that links the distribution centre with the outside processes.

Apart from the afore mentioned processes, value added services are more and more often performed within distribution centres (von der Gracht 2008). They are offered in addition to the core services, and depend on individual customer requests. Therefore, they vary a lot and are not very standardised. One example for such a service would be the building of display pallets.

Further on, every distribution centre needs to fulfil several administrative processes. These can also be linked to the material handling and are referred to as overhead processes. One example for overhead processes are strategic and operational planning.

Due to the functions of the distribution centre described in Section 2.1.1, the number of different goods which are handled in a distribution warehouse is usually very extensive. On the other hand, quantities per order line (articles with same article number) are rather small. This often results in a complex and cost intensive order-picking process (Rouwenhorst et al. 2000, 518-519). Even though Rouwenhorst et al. (2000, 518-519) only mention the order-picking, subsequent processes like packing, for instance, are very complex due to the variance in goods and orders as well. This often leads to "unique" packages in packing, which make efficient operations difficult. With this thesis, we want to contribute to handle this challenge and to be able to structure this process in order to make it more efficient.

2.2 Packing

After presenting an overview of the processes in a distribution centre and how packing is embedded within these, we now focus on packing. Unfortunately, literature on packing seems to be very general and superficial. Sometimes, terms are not defined or even used in different ways. In this section, we want to discuss relevant terms and define how we use them. Further, we want to use this section to give an overview of packing in general and then focus on packing in distribution centres explicitly. There, we want to show differences and commonalities.

2.2.1 Packing in General

According to ASTMD 996 (9), packing can be defined as "the selection or construction of the shipping container and assembling of items or packages therein, including any necessary blocking, bracing, or cushioning, weatherproofing, exterior strapping, and marking of shipping container for identification of contents." Bowersox, Closs and Cooper (2010, 269) add that individual products or parts are typically grouped into cartons, bags, bins, or barrels to avoid damage and allow efficient handling. DIN 55405 (120) defines packing as part of the packing process, where the good is combined with the packaging (packing material and aids) to a package manually or with the aid of packing machines, equipment and devices.

Why is packing necessary? Commonly, different purposes to use packaging are distinguished, whereas terms can vary. Jünemann and Schmidt (2000, 8) and ten Hompel et al. (2007, 6) identify the following functions of the packaging which themselves define requirements for the packaging:

- Protective function (e.g. hardly flammable, stable),
- Storage and transportation function (e.g. stable, bundling),
- Sales function (e.g. economic, informative),
- Identification and information function (e.g. informative, distinguishable) and
- Application function (e.g. easy to open, recyclable).

As we take a closer look at distribution centres, we focus on the purpose that packages are necessary to transport the product from the point of production to the point of use (Arnold et al. 2008, 696).

2.2 Packing

Effectiveness requires stack-ability, standardisation, easy handling, automation friendliness, and unitization of the units (Jünemann and Schmidt 2000, 9). Besides, it is not only necessary to protect the good from transportation hazards, but also to protect the environment from risks of transporting the good (Rummler and Schutt 1991, 90).

Depending on one or more of the functions introduced above, different types of packaging, usually three, are distinguished (cf. Bundesministerium für Umwelt, Naturschutz und Reaktorsicherheit (2008, §3 (1)), Arnold et al. (2008, 697), Hellström and Saghir (2007, 11), ten Hompel et al. (2007, 11), Gustafsson et al. (2005, 3), Saghir (2004, 7), Lee and Lye (2003, 183), Livingstone and Sparks (1994, 16)):

First, goods are packed into the 'primary packaging', which is also called consumer or sales packaging. It is the direct wrapping around a product that the final customer uses to transport or until he consumes the good.

Sometimes, sales packages of the same type are bundled in order to ease handling for goods that are sold on a self-service basis, to prevent from theft, or for advertising purposes. This process of 'bundling' identical packages is being referred to as 'secondary', outer, industry, or multi-unit packaging.

In order to facilitate movement and handling, and to protect goods in transit, finally, transport packaging or 'tertiary packaging' is used. Goods or bundles are packed on pallets, in containers, on crates or in corrugated containers.

2.2.2 Packing in Distribution Centres

Packing which is done in distribution centres in order to bundle a customer order as described in Section 2.1 can be classified as transport or tertiary packaging. This is because its purpose is to protect goods from transportation hazards. The packing unit in a distribution centre usually consists of different types of products (Johnsson 1998, 139), but the term tertiary packaging is frequently used for transport packaging of a single type of goods (cf. Weiblen and Brcincr 2012, 201). Hence, clarification is needed.

Shipping unit or shipping package is widely used in literature for the resulting unit in a distribution centre. This term is not systematised according to, or associated with, the types of packaging (primary, secondary, tertiary) which were introduced in Section 2.2.1. We suggest grouping it as part of tertiary packaging, as the transportation protection and the bundling is the main purpose, but subdivide tertiary packaging according to Figure 2.2.

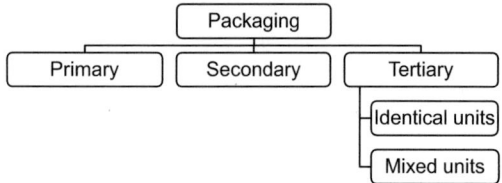

Figure 2.2: Different types of packaging

The term shipping unit will be used in this work to describe the resulting package of the packing process in distribution centres. In order to create this shipping unit, customer ordered goods are bundled to form bigger units (Vahrenkamp 2007, 331). If the shipping unit is broken down and the packaging is removed from goods, the characteristics of the good do not change (DIN 55510-2, 5).

This can only be reached when packing piece goods, which is the standard case in distribution centres. The items can be packaged or not, they might have different shape, and consist of one or several materials (Martin 2009, 62). Bulk goods, liquids or gases are filled into containers beforehand which are then handled as piece goods (Martin 2009, 59 and Großmann and Kaßmann 2007, 17).

The outer layer of a shipping unit can be a corrugated or reusable container, a pallet, a roll container or a freight container (Gudehus 2011, 419, 920). Often, a loading device is used to build the unit (ten Hompel and Schmidt 2010, 23).

As already mentioned, the idea of having shipping units is to make transportation more effective and thereby reduce costs. Having only one unit means fewer handling and identification steps in the supply chain (Pfohl

2010, 141). Other advantages of shipping units are the standardisation of the form and measures as well as stackability (Vahrenkamp 2007, 331).

In this thesis, we want to focus on packing in distribution centres. We can summarise that (tertiary) packaging often refers to the packing of products or the bundling of identical units (for transportation purposes). The typical scenario for packing in distribution centres, however, is a large variety of goods packed together for one customer order, with the purpose to simplify and secure transport. Therefore, in this thesis we refer to the process as packing and to the resulting unit as shipping unit.

2.3 Cycle Times

As we want to determine cycle times for packing in distribution centres, we also want to have a closer look on the field of cycle times. Accordingly, we start by examining definitions of cycle time and their use cases before we give an overview and have a closer look at cycle times for picking in distribution centres, as this should be the closest case to packing in distribution centres. This is part of the basis to determine cycle times for packing in Chapter 6.1.

2.3.1 Definition and Purpose

There are a lot of different approaches to define cycle times. Sometimes, they are related to a specific case like picking for example, sometimes they are more general. To summarise, we start with the definition given in FEM 9851 (1), which is rather simple: "The cycle time is the duration of a motion sequence." Großeschallau (1984, 38) and VDI 2516 (3) title this motion sequence as an operating cycle and add that an operating cycle is a combination of single operations which have been sequenced and are repeated cyclically. VDI 3646 (2) complements that the operation cycle needs to be exactly defined. Further, the cycle time includes productive as well as unproductive times (Arnold and Furmans 2009, 197) and is the reciprocal of the throughput (ten Hompel and Heidenblut 2011, 321).

To summarise the aspects, we state and use the following definition throughout this work:

The cycle time is the duration of a motion sequence. This motion sequence is exactly defined and repeated cyclically. It is the reciprocal of the throughput.

We will see later on, in Section 2.3.3, that this definition might be applied to manual as well as automated processes.

Cycle times can be used to determine the performance of a system (Großeschallau 1984, 38). Usually, mean cycle times, which represent the mean value of the operating cycles (VDI 2516, 4), are used for that purpose. Analytical methods can be used to calculate them in many cases (ten Hompel et al. 2011, 127). For planning, also peaks have to be considered (Lippolt 2003, 55), which usually is done after calculating mean values and with so called worst-case scenarios (cf. VDI 3646, 2). Apart from planning and replanning, cycle times are used to optimise and analyse performance (FEM 9851, 1).

2.3.2 Overview and Use Cases

Following the definition of cycle times in general, we want to give an overview of existing cycle times for specific cases and how they are structured.

To calculate cycle times, durations of single operations are added and possible overlays are taken into account (Großeschallau 1984, 38). Generally, Großeschallau (1984, 38) distinguishes four possible cases for operations duration:

1. Path-independent shares with constant duration,
2. Path-independent shares with variable duration,
3. Path-dependent shares with constant duration and
4. Path-dependent shares with variable duration.

2.3 Cycle Times

Path-dependent shares are related, for instance, to a picker who needs to travel from one picking location to another, and path-independent to the actual grasping. Großeschallau (1984, 38) states that in case 1 and 3 durations need to be measured or calculated only once. For the others, mean cycle times must be calculated or determined by using a measured distribution. In these cases, one has to distinguish between random durations with endless possibilities, and deterministic durations with endless or finite possibilities with different frequency of occurrence.

Borcherdt (1994, 32) does not distinguish path dependency and derives his common cycle time formula as:

$$t_{cycle} = t_{variable} + t_{constant} \qquad (2.1)$$

As examples for variable parts, he mentions travel times, which are influenced by strategies, positions of the served locations, maximum travel speed, acceleration and deceleration of the respective system. Whereas takeovers of units, times for positioning, switching and checking have a constant duration, and are usually referred to as dwell times.

As the average cycle time is the reciprocal of the throughput, we should consider calculations of throughput as well, as a further possibility to calculate average cycle times. For throughput, REFA (1991, 16, 21) distinguishes between execution, intermediate and additional times. Execution times refer to the actual processing, intermediate times to planned storage and transport, and additional times to time allowances, which are usually calculated in percent. This differentiation focuses more on structuring the purpose of time needed than on differences of properties of time shares.

These formulas are very generic as one only focuses on the purpose of the time necessary and the other one only differentiates between variable and constant parts. Therefore, we want to have a closer look at cycle times of different technical implementations, see how they are structured and compare them with the two different approaches to structure cycle times: either with the focus on the purpose of the time necessary, or differentiating between variable and constant time shares.

VDI 3646 (2-8) for continuous conveyors reveals that there is no common formula for conveyors. But, in general, switching, dwell, positioning, lifting, or turning times are added to handling time, depended on the technical realisation. At the same time, this shows that there is no common definition of dwell time, as most of the additional times mentioned above are referred to as dwell time by Borcherdt (1994, 32) and summarised as part of the constant time shares.

For piece good conveyors, VDI 3978 (12) distinguishes between travel time and time for acceleration and deceleration. Again, this is in contrast to Borcherdt (1994, 32), who subsumes acceleration and deceleration as part of the travel time. VDI 3978 (2) adds that if operation cycles differ, it is useful to define a 'typical' cycle in order to dimensioning and control the system.

For non-continuous conveyors, which can also be regarded as transports, Fischer and Dittrich (2004, 74) remark as well that the first step is to define a reference cycle. For transportation in general, they make a distinction between the load or transportation cycle, which includes pick-up and delivery of the good as well as transport, and the empty trip, which is necessary to reach the next or the same pick-up point. This definition better matches the general definition of REFA (1991, 16, 21), as it focuses on transport for a purpose and the empty trip which is necessary to get back.

Römisch (2011, 171) uses cycle times to calculate the number of industrial trucks needed in a system, and distinguishes between travel time and time needed for pick-up and delivery, whereas travel time can be assumed as variable, and pick-up and delivery as constant. Gudehus (2006, 315) also focuses on transportation, especially on round trips. He identifies three parts: travel time, stop time and base time. Here, the travel time can be seen as the variable time share and the base time as the constant time share, as this is needed to pick-up and deliver. He does not further detail the stop time, but as there is no formula given to calculate it, it can be assumed that it is of constant nature as well. Therefore, both relate more to the definition of Borcherdt (1994, 32).

For cranes, VDI 2195 (2-3) differs between the load cycle and the empty trip, as Fischer and Dittrich (2004, 74) did for transport. So all kinds of crane movements like lifting, crane travelling, trolley travelling, lowering, turning, positioning and waiting times (VDI 4446, 6) are classified either in one of the two or both categories, depending on the purpose of the specific movement.

2.3 Cycle Times

We can summarise that both possibilities to structure cycle times, the one focusing on the purpose of the time necessary and the one differentiating between variable and constant time shares, are used to model cycle times for different cases. Both have to be kept in mind when deriving formulas for packing in Chapter 6. The cycle times discussed above did not only focus on processes in distribution centres. In the following, we therefore want to take a closer look at calculating cycle times for picking in distribution centres to figure out analogies that are relevant for determining cycle times for packing in Chapter 6.

2.3.3 Picking

If we take a closer look at cycle times for picking, we realise that the definition of Borcherdt (1994, 32), including variable and constant time shares, covers most of the formulas. Usually one part, the variable part, represents the travel time and the other part is either referred to as dwell time (Gudehus 1973), constant time (VDI 4418), handover time (Schumann 2008) or loading time (Atz and Günthner 2011). Sometimes the constant part is not regarded as one, but as two parts: Seemüller (2005) differs between the cycle for the load handling device and the set-up time. VDI 2516 is similar: the load transfer, and the positioning or respond time is differentiated. Conversely, VDI 3561 subdivides the variable part into travel and acceleration time.

In the following, we have a closer look at the two main components, travel and dwell time, how important they are, which process steps are included and how they are measured.

The total cycle time for picking is mainly influenced by the travel time (Gudehus 2011, 622). As this time component is variable, calculation formulas depend on the technical system and the strategies used (Sadowsky 2007, 48). The different systems resulting from combining these two characteristics are treated by the authors already mentioned (an overview is given in ten Hompel and Hömberg 2008). Time calculation for the different systems is mainly dependent on velocity, which can be characterised by functions in an appropriate accuracy (Gudehus 1973, 56-59). The technical data used for calculation depends on the specific system in place (FEM 9.851 1978, 3).

The dwell time can be measured on site, or by using predetermined motion time systems, like MTM or Work-Factor (Gudehus 2011, 739). In order to determine this time share, it can be further subdivided, as mentioned earlier. For example Gudehus (1973, 46) distinguishes between base, picking and set-up time. We want to have a closer look at these components subsequently.

The base time includes time shares for taking the picking list, sorting its contents according to strategies, picking of a loading aid, delivery of the aid and/or the goods, as well as marking them according to the destination (Gudehus 1973, 55). For mechanical implementations, base time sometimes is not distinguished, but alternatively a time for the mast to stop swinging is included (Lippolt 2003, 55). For manual systems, it is the time that a picker spends before and after picking at the base station. The time components included in the base time vary, as for example the sorting of the order is not necessarily done by the picker, but might have been done before printing the list. The time spent at the base station needs to be measured or determined as mentioned above, and is then divided by the number of positions (ten Hompel et al. 2011, 133), as the cycle time is usually measured per picking position, but base time occurs only once per picking list. Waiting times at the base station, for instance for the next order, are not part of the base time (Gudehus 2011, 741).

The picking time includes not only time shares required to reach for the good, to grasp and transport it until the release, but can also include labelling or marking of products as well as breaking provision units open (Gudehus 1973, 46). For mechanical systems, picking time is also referred to as 'load handling time' (cf. Gudehus 1973, 51). In Gudehus (2011, 739) cutting, weighing and measuring are added as further operations. The picking time is influenced mainly by the height, depth and angle which need to be bridged (ten Hompel et al. 2011, 133). Gudehus (2011, 739) adds picking quantity per position, volume and weight of the unit as influencing parameters. Empirical data indicates picking times between two and ten seconds per unit, depending on volume and weight (Gudehus 2011, 741). For mechanical systems, picking time can be assumed as the time it takes the load handling device to transfer the load, which depends on the velocity, acceleration and distance between load and device (Lippolt 2003, 55).

2.3 Cycle Times

The set-up time is a time during which no change of the system can be realised externally (Gudehus 1973, 53). It includes time for information processing (reading, searching, identification, coding, typing or documentation), for positioning (going up, getting off, aligning, supporting and promoting, back and forward movements) and handling (set up of packaging, closing of packaging, coding, labelling, taking an empty loading aid, moving or opening units in the shelf) as well as waiting times (e.g. waiting for supply, for information, for congestions) (Gudehus 2011, 737-738). Comparing both books of Gudehus, one realises that taking an empty loading aid is included in the base time in Gudehus (1973), whereas it is included in the set-up time in Gudehus (2011). So, it is either not clearly defined, or the idea of how to structure these times changed over the years. Typical empirical durations for manually operated picking systems are one to two seconds per position, and for automated systems half a second to one second are assumed (Gudehus 2011, 627). Times are influenced by the working conditions, spatial setting, form, content and quality of information provided, as well as attention and experience of the picker (Gudehus 2011, 738).

Other times, such as the time for transporting goods to the next area, are not considered, as they do not influence the picking as long as it does not result in waiting times for the picking process (Gudehus 1973, 12).

The total cycle time is calculated by adding the components, but as mentioned before it is necessary to consider parallel operations. Whenever operations can be executed in parallel, the longer lasting one has to be chosen (Gudehus 2011, 739). As results of the cycle times should be mean values, it is also necessary to look at similar picking orders, otherwise variation is too big. Because input parameters already vary by ten percent, it is an approximate calculation and an exact calculation is not possible (Gudehus 1973, 44-45). To give an example, travel times for an one dimensional picking system are calculated as an integral and not as summation on all shelves, which would be the exact way for this problem (Gudehus 1973, 59-60).

In order to calculate the proper performance of a system, factors for availability and usability have to be considered. The first factor includes times for unproductive shares, like technical downtimes, personal need allowance, and non-picking related secondary work (Gudehus 2011, 744). The second factor covers times for waiting due to congestions, for information or supply and can be calculated for the specific system using queuing theory (Gudehus 2011, 745). Here again, Gudehus (2011) does not clearly mention how waiting times should be taken into account: either as a part of the set-up time (cf. page 738) or by including a factor when calculating the effective performance (cf. page 735, 744-748).

In all, we have seen that for picking purposes, the cycle time is divided into a variable and a constant time share, as Borcherdt (1994) suggests. The constant time share is further subdivided into base, picking and set-up time, and the sub-processes of picking are allocated among them according to their characteristics. Variable time shares are calculated using an approximative formula, constant time shares need to be determined by using predetermined motion time systems or by measuring.

3 Related work

Chapter 2 introduced processes within a distribution centre and discussed further topics relevant for this thesis to provide a solid level of background knowledge. This chapter more specifically looks into extant literature, which provides knowledge about calculating packing times in distribution centres. We identify three scientific works which are particularly relevant, show promising approaches and highlight differences and similarities.

3.1 Design for Manual Packaging

In their paper 'Design for Manual Packaging', Lee and Lye (2003) take a closer look not on packing in distribution centres, but on packaging of products after manufacturing. They develop a methodology to assess manual packaging operations. For this purpose, standard times are derived for common operations and recommendations for the design of packaging lines are given. As mentioned, their paper focuses on manual workplaces for product packaging only. In contrast, we aim to study packing in distribution centres, where the packing process varies more because shipping units differ from one and another (cf. Section 2.2). However, some of the steps taken in the paper of Lee and Lye (2003) are interesting for packing in distribution centres and the development of cycle times.

In order to improve packaging of products, Lee and Lye (2003, 166) structure the process according to necessary steps and identify packaging material which is used within each step. They classify the material according to the impact on handling into four groups: if one, two or three hands without machines are needed, or two hands with the aid of a machine, which is an interesting idea to qualitatively represent the effort. To be able to determine an analytical formula for the packing time, the approach of structuring the process into steps will be absolutely necessary as the complexity of the process as a whole is too high. Also, an overview of options of process design and possibly used material is essential, to be able to consider different scenarios and still have a common formula. To identify time relevant parameters, their influences need to be determined.

For the operations identified in their paper, Lee and Lye (2003, 168-175) derive standard times. For this purpose, they measure 20 cycles of each operation, either on site or in a test environment, and calculate mean times. The mean time is then referred to as 'normal time'. The normal time is additionally rated according to the skills of the operator, and a further factor for personal, fatigue and delay allowances is included in their formula. The statistical validity of the stated values is problematic, because no variances are provided and it is unclear whether 20 measured cycles are enough for a reasonable level of confidence. In this thesis, we will need time values as well, either to determine the influence of parameters or to calculate case studies. In contrast to Lee and Lye (2003), we will use values given by standard methods like predetermined motion time systems, as mentioned for picking in Gudehus (2011, 739). These time values have already been statistically verified.

In the paper of Lee and Lye (2003, 172-175), 'standard times' resulting from the adjustments of 'normal times' are differentiated by the size of the packaging unit, the type of material, the rotational symmetry and movements, as these parameters influence the time needed to execute the packaging process. As we want to determine the influencing parameters of packing, we need to consider the above given parameters, in order to be able to judge which parameters and specifications need to be included for packing in distribution centres.

As indicated, some of the thoughts and methods presented in Lee and Lye (2003) may prove helpful for our thesis. On the other hand, the focus of their work is different, as they look at product packaging with identical products. In a distribution centre scenario, in contrast, we cannot predict which combination of goods needs to be packed.

3.2 Process Cost Model for Manual Packing Workplaces

In her thesis 'Process Cost Model for Manual Packing Workplaces', Dzeik (2008) develops a model to calculate packing cost for manual or partly automated workplaces. For this purpose, she first analyses processes to be able to get times, to allocate costs according to where they incurred afterwards. She validates her model with an analysis of two reference cases. Even though she does not exclude packing in distribution centres and mentions it as one possible case, both reference cases are product packaging in the automotive industry context. Packing of large loading units, especially with varying product mixes, is not included. In her conclusions she describes the resulting calculating algorithm as complex, which is due to the necessity to obtain precise figures in order to share costs according to where they are incurred.

Another difference is that calculations in Dzeik (2008) are an a posteriori evaluation and we are looking for calculation models to support planning, so we do not have figures from existing processes. The formula we want to determine should be general and valid for cases typically found in distribution centres, including automated processes and large unit loads. As a result, a general structure is necessary, as input parameters in a priori planning will not be as precise as for existing systems (Gudehus 1973, 44-45). Even though Dzeik's thesis differs in focus, it has to be considered. The following key elements should be kept in mind.

In Chapter 2.2, Dzeik (2008) discusses organisational differences between packing workplaces. She describes their arrangements, how they are supplied, and how a workplace can be designed. Her idea is that the possible organisational structure depends on the packing task which needs to be performed and on the number of packing workplaces, which has to be set (Dzeik 2008, 19). She treats the number of workplaces as given, but this is exactly one of the points which this thesis will focus on: we want to provide formulas to determine the time needed for packing and thus to derive how many workplaces are needed. Thereby, the set-up of the packing area is not a given, as the main purpose is to use cycle times for planning and to compare alternative possibilities.

In order to distinguish and characterise packing tasks, Dzeik (2008, 30-32) considers different criteria. One is the arrangement of materials and devices, the second is the supply and provision of packages and the last is the amount and the composition of goods. As she argues, only the last criterion seems applicable to her purposes and subdivides it further. Finally, she distinguishes between packing one or several goods. For 'several goods', four different cases are considered:

- Several, but identical goods,
- Re-packing, the packing of already packaged products into a transport packaging,
- Several, not identical goods in an identical combination, and
- Several, not identical goods in varying combinations.

According to these categories, standard processes and workplace layouts are defined. The process of packing in distribution centres rarely includes packing of a single good and is usually of the last category of several goods in varying combinations (cf. Dzeik 2008, 45). For this case, seven types of packing workplaces are differentiated. Dzeik (2008, 29) emphasises that it is neither possible nor useful to describe all possibilities to design packing workplaces and gives minimal design guidelines. She then focuses on some of these workplace types and fixes process steps according to the respective type and the fixed layout. For this thesis, we need to consider these process steps and enhance them, so that other packing tasks which are part of packing in distribution centres, such as the packing of pallets, fit in as well. In addition, we need to check if the last category can be further subdivided to pay respect to different amounts of effort required to perform the packing task. But in line with Dzeik (2008), we will not research on the design of packing workplaces and their differences, as this would exceed the limits of this work.

Later on in her thesis, a process chain for packing, independent from the above mentioned categories, is given and subdivided (Dzeik 2008, 88-99). For these sub-processes, typical values are determined with the method of MTM-SD based on mainly two influencing parameters (Dzeik 2008, 118-134). To give an example, time required for setting up corrugated containers depends on the type of the used container and its size (Dzeik 2008, 121-123). She identified the relevant parameters in a previous work

3.2 Process Cost Model for Manual Packing Workplaces

by using an analysis of variance (Dzeik and Picker 2003). It would certainly be possible to calculate process times for the given layouts and process steps or individual combinations of sub-process by combining different parts of her thesis. But this is possible only for manual packing and with a focus on corrugated containers. Also, many process steps are only relevant for product packaging and not necessary in a distribution centre environment, where goods that need special protection are usually already packed in an appropriate product packaging. However, we definitely need to deduce a typical process chain for packing in distribution centres as well, before we are able to identify relevant influencing parameters and can determine cycle time formulas. The relevance of the influencing parameters could be evaluated as in Dzeik (2008), by using an analysis of variance.

It is hard to describe the relevance of Dzeik (2008) for this work, as in some cases we need to detail it (for instance, packing in distribution centres is only briefly discussed, as it only corresponds to one of her cases). In other cases we need to generalise it, because we want to determine a general calculation formula which, for example, shall not restrict the application to manual processes. To give another example with regard to cycle times: On the one hand, we need to identify and discard all parts which are relevant for product packaging only. On the other hand, we need to identify how we could include pallet packing cases, for instance.

In other words, we definitely need to consider her work, as one of her cases is packing in distribution centres, and also her way of proceeding will affect this thesis. It is certainly necessary to structure the packing process in distribution centres with its characteristics and to identify and consider influencing parameters. But as the focus in her thesis is not only on packing in distribution centre and this case is just one of many, it seems to be not detailed enough. Further, only the packing of corrugated containers is regarded, which is just one possible task in a distribution centre.

3.3 Development of Optimised Operation Strategies for Sorting Systems

In his thesis 'Development of Optimised Operation Strategies for Sorting Systems', Radtke (2000) focuses on consolidation systems and sorters. As part of these systems, he enquiries packing workplaces as destinations at the end of sorters because they might affect the sorting system as a limiting component (Radtke 2000, 133). Based on several assumptions he calculates time requirements for packing, to be able to dimension the sorter and its necessary number of destinations. He divides the packing time into time shares for waiting, packing, travelling as well as base time and time to finish the packing process. For the waiting time calculation, he uses queuing theory, other parts are partly based on assumptions or calculations. As this system, with a combination of sorting and packing, is one of the technical implementations found in distribution centres, we have to consider this approach.

Radtke (2000, 72) mentions that he simplified packing time calculation by using assumptions, as packing is not his major concern. Further, he mentions that layouts as well as strategies vary too much to have one detailed, general valid calculation formula for packing. In order to predict the maximum performance of a packing system as part of the sorting system, Radtke (2000, 72) proceeds based on the following assumptions:

- The packing workplaces are arranged in a line and the distance between workplaces is constant.
- The working areas of packers are of the same size.
- The order in which the destinations of the sorter need to be visited by the packer is given.
- Within one sorting batch every destination is visited only once.
- In order to consider travel times, more than one destination has to be assigned to a packer.
- Packing time per item is constant.
- All packers perform equal.

3.3 Development of Optimised Operation Strategies for Sorting Systems

- Personal need allowances are not considered.
- Packing of an order must start after sorting is completed.
- Distances need to be at a minimum.

As one of the possible realisations of packing in distribution centres, this case of packing at a destination of a sorter has to be considered for the general formula determined in this thesis as well. It needs to be noted, that this is one specific case of packing and therefore assumptions are very restricting, like the arrangement in a line or that a packer needs to travel between workplaces. However, it might be necessary for us as well to make assumptions in order to determine a general formula later on.

In the following, we give a brief overview of his calculations in order to determine packing time, which are relevant for our thesis as well.

Radtke (2000) calculates the packing performance as a quotient of the number of parts and the time needed by packers for processing, which he calls 'batch tact':

$$\mu_{P1,T} = \frac{m_{P1,T}}{T_{BT}} \qquad (3.1)$$

$m_{P1,T}$ is the number of items needed to be packed in one sorting batch by one packer. T_{BT}, the process time for one packer, is calculated as follows:

$$T_{BT} = T_{P1,Wait} + \sum_{i=1}^{m_{P1,T}} T_{Pack,Item\ i} \\ + \sum_{j=1}^{m_{P1,A}} \left(T_{Travel,ES\ j} + T_{Base,ES\ j} + T_{Finish,ES\ j} \right) \qquad (3.2)$$

with

$T_{P1,Wait}$ unproductive times (waiting for items),

$T_{Pack,Item\ i}$ time to pick item i of the sorting batch and pack it into shipping container or on pallet,

$m_{P1,A}$ number of orders of a sorting batch which have to be packed by one packer,

$T_{Travel,ES\ j}$ travel time for distance to destination j of the sorter,

$T_{Base,ES\ j}$ preparing work at destination j of the sorter and

$T_{Finish,ES\ j}$ finishing work at destination j of the sorter.

Subsequently, he simplifies Formula 3.2 according to his assumptions:

$$T_{BT} = T_{P1,Wait} + m_{P1,T} \cdot T_{Pack,Item} \\ + m_{P1,A} \cdot (T_{Base,ES} + T_{Finish,ES}) + \sum_{j=1}^{m_{P1,A}} T_{Travel,ES\ j} \quad (3.3)$$

He assumes that the values of $m_{P1,T}$, $T_{Pack,Item}$, $m_{P1,A}$, $T_{Base,ES}$ and $T_{Finish,ES}$ are known, whereas he wants to calculate the unproductive time shares of the waiting time $T_{P1,Wait}$ and the travel time $T_{Travel,ES\ j}$ (Radtke 2000, 73).

The travel time is only relevant if the packer serves more than one destination of the sorter, because space at the destination is usually so limited that walking is not considered possible (Radtke 2000, 73). Radtke calculates travel times for two scenarios: either the packer finishes one order before moving to the next destination or interrupts work and changes between destinations. For the first case, he finally assumes the following travel time with the assumption that maximum velocity is reached in any case (Radtke 2000, 75):

$$T_{Travel,ESj} = \frac{v_{walk}}{a_b} + \frac{\bar{l}_{(j)}}{v_{walk}} \\ = \frac{v_{walk}}{a_b} + \frac{d}{v_{walk}} \cdot (\frac{1}{n^2} + \frac{1}{n}) \cdot \sum_{i=1}^{n} |i-j| \quad (3.4)$$

with

v_{walk} velocity of the packer (which he assumes with one meter per second)

a_b acceleration/deceleration of the packer,

$\bar{l}_{(j)}$ mean distance to destination j,

d distance between two neighbouring destinations,

n number of destinations served by one packer, which equals $m_{P1,A}$ if destinations are only occupied once during one sorting batch,

3.3 Development of Optimised Operation Strategies for Sorting Systems

i a destination of the sorter and

j the neighbouring destination of the sorter.

The sum of travel times for the process time (cf. Equation 3.3) can then be simplified to:

$$\sum_{j=1}^{n} T_{Travel,ESj} = n \cdot \frac{v_{walk}}{a_b} + \frac{d}{3 \cdot v_{walk}} \cdot (n^2 + n - \frac{1}{n} - 1) \qquad (3.5)$$

Radtke (2000) tries to calculate the waiting time using a $M|D|1$ queuing model, among others. At the end of his considerations, he concludes that the potential use of the results is only very restricted, as the system never reaches steady state (Radtke 2000, 83-91). He does not use the results of this calculation further in his thesis.

In other words, we consider Radtke (2000) within this thesis because the special case of packing at destinations of a sorter is analysed in his work and it is one scenario in distribution centres. While doing so, we need to keep in mind that his calculation aims to calculate the maximum performance at a packing workplace, as he wants to calculate the performance of a sorting system, and not mean values represented by mean cycle times. Also, Radtke (2000) only considers the packing of a whole sorting batch, whereas cycle times for packing should focus on a single packing operation. Although the level of detail and focus of his calculations therefore are a bit different, undoubtedly parts could be used later on. Especially, calculations of travel times seem to be promising. But it must be kept in mind that he made particular assumptions, mentioned above, relating to the sorting system. For example, concerning the travelling of the packer between the destinations or the layout.

4 Defining the Packing Process

As we have found in Chapter 2.1, packing is integrated in up- and downstream processes in a distribution centre which also includes transports between processes or supply of materials (cf. Figure 4.1). In order to analyse packing processes in distribution centres, and to determine cycle time formulas for one process, it does not make sense to consider all processes within a distribution centre (e.g. receiving and storing process for packaging material) and their interfaces with each other. There are too many dependencies and the variety is too big to be handled in a first investigation of the process in focus. In order to calculate the time impact of packing, we only focus on packing relevant activities, which we will derive in the following.

We want to look at the 'primary supply' for packing, which includes the flow from a supply area to the packing workplace and the supply of shipping units from the workplace to a provision area as well as any transport of goods within the area. In contrast, 'secondary supply' for supply with consumables, such as packaging material, is considered out of the scope as these processes vary too much (analogue to Gudehus 2011, 744). Secondary supplies are transported from different areas within the distribution centre to the packing area, automatically or manually, with or without devices, in one or several cycles, in- or excluding intermediate steps. So, we can summarise that these transports highly depend on the local settings and therefore cannot be part of a general analysis. This secondary supply and transport between the areas is sine qua non for the packing process (Bleisch et al. 2011, 185).

Figure 4.1, following Lolling (2003, 7), who investigated picking systems, shows the packing process and how it is embedded in the system of a distribution centre. As it is outlined, the focus of this thesis is the packing process. This process can be investigated from the main perspectives:

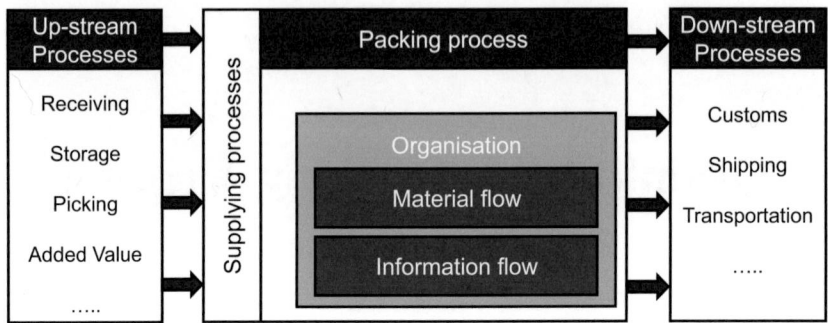

Figure 4.1: Sub-systems of the packing process (by analogy to Lolling 2003, 7)

organisation, material flow and information system. This structuring is also according to VDI 3590-1 (2) and can be transferred to packing. We will focus on these three sub-systems of packing in the following sections, starting with material flow as the information flow only supports the material flow and the higher-level organisation refers to both.

4.1 Material Flow

DIN 30781-1 (2) defines material flow as the chain of all processes necessary for gaining, working and processing as well as distributing goods within defined areas. Arnold and Furmans (2009, 11) categorise the major technical processes in material flow into the generic terms: process, assemble, check, handle, convey (transport), store (buffer), accumulate, distribute, sort and pack.

We use process chains according to Kuhn (1995) and VDI 3600 in order to structure the material flow of the packing process. Alternatively to the process chains, we also investigated event-driven process chains (EPKs) and UML activity diagrams as these methods are also commonly used to map processes. Event-driven process chains turned out to be inappropriate as each step needs to be referred to twice (once as function and once as event), which leads to an unnecessary complexity in our case. UML

4.1 Material Flow

activity diagrams have the feature of showing decision alternatives, but as we want to show packing as a general process and do not need to map specific technical alternatives for instance, it seems to be inappropriate here. Further, it would be adopted from another discipline (cf. Nyhuis and Wiendahl 2012, 190). Process chains, in contrast, are used as a tool in logistics to illustrate complex processes in order to make them transparent (VDI 3600, 23), and we will use these in this work.

When deriving process chains, the main process (here packing) is subdivided in so called sub-processes, which are bundled activities with a common result (Michel et al. 2004, 231-232). For packing, this would be for example the securing as a sub-process, where taping and strapping the unit contribute to the result of a secured shipping unit. The sub-processes themselves contribute to the final result of the main process (VDI 3600, 2).

In order to distinguish sub-processes, we reviewed literature on packing processes (Bleisch et al. 2011, 171, Pfohl 2010, 140, Günthner and Lammer 2009, 77, Dzeik 2008, 38-40, Crostack et al. 2007, 36-37, VDI 4490, 9, Lee and Lye 2003, 183, Frazelle 2002, 230, Radtke 2000, 57, Menk 1998, 122, Lange 1998, 104, as well as Heinz and Olbrich 1989, 122) for relevance to packing within distribution centres. As the detailing level of the described packing processes proved to be very ambiguous, we analysed and grouped packing steps according to their result. This proceeding is required for sub-processes of process chains according to the definition of VDI 3600 (2) and Michel et al. (2004, 231-232) like mentioned above. Figure 4.2 gives an overview of the resulting sub-processes.

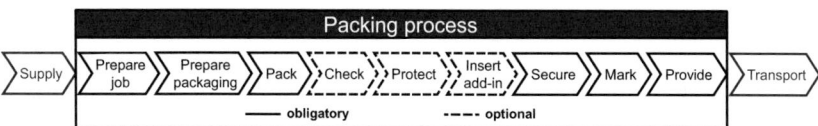

Figure 4.2: Packing process steps of the material flow system

The packing process shown should be universally valid, as we do not want to analyse a specific distribution centre but packing processes in general. Naturally, some highly specific cases might not fit into it. We define some sub-processes as obligatory since they are fixed steps in packing for the most cases. Others are optional, because it depends on the circumstances whether they are performed or not. This also applies for the following sub-chapters, where an overview of activities performed within the sub-processes is given. Not necessarily have all activities to be performed in every distribution centre.

4.1.1 Prepare Job

As shown in Figure 4.1, the packing process starts with the handover of the supplying transport from the upstream process. It depends on the local set-up where this supply arrives: either it arrives in a supply area and the packer needs to fetch items from there, or items arrive directly at his workplace. Apart from this, it is necessary to take a hold of, move, position and align items before they can be packed (Günthner and Lammer 2009, 60).

As noticed, it might be necessary to move items in order to pack them. In the best case, the items are provided in the right packing order within reach of the packer, so that moving them is not necessary. However, items are often provided on a picking trolley in a supply area and the packer needs to go there, either to get items from the trolley or the complete trolley including the items. In any case, a packer leaving the packing workplace in order to transport items should be avoided for value-adding purposes (cf. seven wastes, Ohno 2009, 52). Taking a hold of, positioning and orienting an item for packing is part of the packing sub-process (Section 4.1.3).

If not directly provided at the workplace, the packing job needs to be chosen (either randomly or according to existing rules) and in any case identified. Firstly, identification is necessary to provide information on the job. These information are necessary to be able to choose the right packaging, protection or securing material, to check quantity later on in sub-process checking, and to get details on activities, which need to be performed. These details can be displayed with an electronic device and therefore the job is usually scanned. Secondly, identification is necessary to be able to confirm the processing of the packing job.

We include the decisions on the right packaging, protection, and securing in this step. These could be for instance decisions on the proper pallet or corrugated container, on the cushioning material or on the securing method to be used, all depending on the dimensions, weight or fragility of the items. Especially the choice of cushioning material depends on the sensitivity of the product and the level of stress during the transportation process (Lange 1998, 106).

4.1.2 Prepare Packaging

As 'prepare packaging' we summarise all activities necessary to have a package that is ready to be filled (Crostack et al. 2007, 38). The amount of packaging material needed to pack should be stored in reach of the packer, so that he is not required to leave his workplace. The replenishment of material is a separate process and out of scope. We assume here that the material is provided at the workplace.

The packaging has to be taken and positioned, in order to pack the items into it. Typically, this is already an exhaustive description for pallets, however if the packaging is a corrugated container, for example, it has to be set up before it is ready to be filled with items. Setting up is the process of erecting a knocked-down box into a box and includes the end, cover and section closures before the box is filled (ASTM D1974, 2). Another example would be a wire mesh box or a container, which needs to be opened before items can be packed inside. If no standard loading unit is used, preparing the packaging includes the 'assembling' of the loading unit. One example for this would be a self-made half-sized pallet.

4.1.3 Pack

The pack sub-process refers to the actual placing of material into a container for handling, storage and transportation (ASTM D996, 7). The term used differs from primary packaging, where it is usually referred to as filling (Bleisch et al. 2011, 177). The speed and stability that can be reached in this sub-process of packing both depend on the (primary) packaging of the good (cf. Hellström and Saghir 2007, 203).

First, the items have to be grasped before placing and releasing them. As placing already describes, the positioning of items is also part of this sub-process. To assist the packer, packing patterns can be provided. They aim at an optimal unit space usage and especially stacking patterns aim at an inherent stability (Martin 2009, 76). These patterns are mainly used for pallets, which are only efficient if they resist the stress of the succeeding distribution process (Großmann and Kaßmann 2007, 20-21). As mentioned within preparing the job, items might be in a wrong order, for example heavy items need to be packed first. This arranging in proper order is also part of the packing sub-process.

Additionally, in some distribution centres a concept called 'pick and pack' is used. As the name implies, it combines the packing and picking process as items are picked directly into or onto the shipping unit. As Günthner and Lammer (2009, 62) mention, in this case the second grasping, within the sub-process pack, is not necessary. Anyhow, other process steps of packing, like protecting or securing are still required. But in order to calculate the cycle time for the pick and pack method, it is necessary to consider both the picking and packing process at the same time, which is not part of this thesis, but is an interesting topic for further research.

4.1.4 Check

To prevent that a customer receives a wrong amount or types of items, the checking sub-process is very common in distribution centres, even though it cannot be found everywhere (ten Hompel and Schmidt 2010, 52). Often, it is combined with the packing process, as the packer already holds the item in his hands and can rotate it in order to check the item number, for example. Usually identity and amount are checked (cf. Figure 4.3), but also quality and/or volume might be interesting. For this step, it might be necessary to use additional devices or tools, such as a ruler. The checking usually also includes a confirmation of the checked characteristic.

The quantity (and identity) check might be counting, identifying and confirming lines on a packing list, scanning the bar-code of the items or by weighing them (Crostack et al. 2007, 33). Weighing might be faster, but highly relies on the master data being available for the articles and a homogeneous weight of the articles (ten Hompel and Schmidt 2010, 52 and Crostack et al. 2007, 46), as well as differences big enough between the weights of different articles. Even though radio-frequency identification

4.1 Material Flow

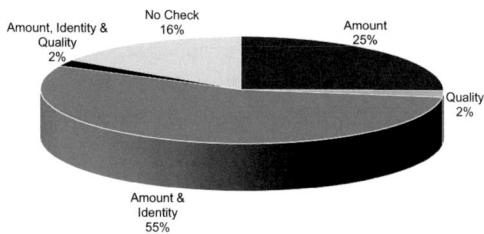

Figure 4.3: Distribution of checking methods, n=80 (Weiblen and Berbig 2011)

(RFID) and image recognition are not very common in distribution centres, an automatic check with these technologies might be possible as well.

4.1.5 Protect

To protect the content of the shipping unit from damages, different techniques can be used. For pallets, mainly securing layers between the packages are added, to prevent them from moving (Großmann and Kaßmann 2007, 21). Goods in shipping containers are usually protected with filling or cushioning material to reduce the effect of externally applied shock or vibration forces (ASTM D996, 5). Often paper pads, air cushions, foam pads or loose fill are used.

The operations necessary for cushioning depend on the material used. The cushioning has to be grasped and inserted into the container. This also applies when items require special protection, such as cooling or if they are electrostatic sensitive, and for the protection material used to guarantee this. Also securing layers need to be grasped and inserted. As before, we assume that this material is provided at the packing workplace and refilling is considered as a separate process. Yet, as cushioning material is very voluminous, it might be necessary to move even at the workplace in order to reach it.

4.1.6 Insert Add-in

Further material might be inserted into or attached to the loading unit in addition to the items, such as invoices, delivery notes, packing lists, flyers, catalogues, giveaways, gifts, data loggers or sensors.

Therefore, they need to be grasped, sometimes it is necessary to fold and put them into an envelope or a bag before inserting them into the loading unit or attaching them to it. Whenever some documents are printed at the packing workplace, the activities associated might also include a manual input to start the print job. As before, we do not consider the provision process here, but assume that add-in materials are provided at the workplace.

4.1.7 Secure

Activities to guarantee a save transport to the internal or external customer include the following (Braun et al. 2010, 49-50):

- Cushioning of a container,
- Closing a container,
- Capping a small load carrier,
- Strapping, stretching or shrink wrapping a loading unit.

We already discussed the cushioning of a container as a means of protecting items inside a loading unit and assumed it as part of the sub-process 'protect' (cf. Section 4.1.5). The other activities stated are part of the sub-process 'secure' and are discussed in the following. Closing of a container as well as putting a cap on a small load carrier are grouped, as activities to perform them are very similar. Here as well, we do not consider the refilling of securing material and assume it is provided at the workplace.

Closing a container, to avoid accidental opening during normal shipment, handling and storage, requires taking the flaps or covers to close the filling and prevent opening (ASTM D1974, 2). Thereafter, closing methods to fix the joint can be used individually or multiple. DIN EN 14053 (7) distinguishes between glueing (hot or cold), taping, stitching and locking.

4.1 Material Flow

Depending on the method, further steps are necessary. To fix the joint of corrugated containers usually tape is used (DIN 55479, 2). This process seals the seam, which also keeps dust and dirt out of the box (Brody and Marsh 1997, 883-884). The tape has to be measured in the right size, so that it overlaps, before it is cut off. It has to be attached centrally, and stuck on top and sides (DIN 55479, 2). To be able to perform these activities, materials as well as tools and supplies for work are necessary, which are assumed to be located at the workplace.

Unit loads are secured in order to protect them from mechanical, climatic and other stresses like theft or manipulation (Bleisch et al. 2011, 455, Arnold et al. 2008, 706). Securing effectively avoids a qualitative, quantitative and material change during storing, transshipping and transporting (VDI 3638, 7). We already discussed the method of inserting securing layers in Section 4.1.5, which is an organisational-technical method (VDI 3968-2, 2). In this sub-chapter we focus on securing of loading units after they have been built. In many cases devices are used for this task. To reduce investments, often several packers share these devices which are located in a central area. As the transport to these places is part of the packing process and not related to transport of supplies, we need to consider it. Therefore, the unit additionally needs to be picked up and placed.

Jansen (2008, 58) states that in 80 percent of securing operations stretch wrapping is used. The most common methods for the remaining 20 percent are strapping and shrink wrapping (ten Hompel and Schmidt 2010, 24, Arnold et al. 2008, 707, Großmann and Kaßmann 2007, 25). As a result, we focus on these three methods. The decision on one of these methods depends on type, weight and size of the packages, the sensitivity against mechanical and climatic stresses, the required performance of the securing process and the integration into up- and down-stream processes, investments as well as purchase and disposal costs (Arnold et al. 2008, 711). Jünemann and Schmidt (2000, 39) and ten Hompel et al. (2007, 47-48) compare the three methods and assess how well they perform regarding influencing parameters. The decision on the securing method is part of the sub-process 'prepare job'.

For stretch wrapping a film is mechanically expanded or widened in order to have continuous tension within the film (VDI 3968-5, 3). This film is then wrapped around the unit load. Operations necessary depend on the differences in stretch wrapping; three kinds are distinguished: stretch convolution, stretch hooding and banding (Arnold et al. 2008, 708 and VDI 3968-5, 3). Usually, stretch wrapping refers to the stretch convolution variant, where the film is fixed at the pallet and wound around the unit load until the top is reached (Arnold et al. 2008, 709).

Strapping is used for bundles and bales as well as for shipping units (ASTM D996, 11). If the unit is heavier than 50 kg, strapping should be used in addition to adhesive tape (Eschke 2005, 77). The strap is put around the unit load before it is tensioned. Thereafter, the overlapping ends need to be fastened and the remaining strap can be cut off (VDI 3968-3, 8). This process is repeated, as it is necessary to have several straps to bind together the loading unit (Arnold et al. 2008, 708). The material of the strap can be steel, nylon, polypropylene, or polyester and to fasten it either heating or sealing are used (Brody and Marsh 1997, 860). Additionally, protection material for the edges can be used below the strappings.

Shrink wrapping is possible by means of a special film (Arnold et al. 2008, 710-711). Tension inherent in the film is set free by heating it. Therefore, the loading unit needs to be wrapped with film, which is usually hood-shaped and put as cover over the unit, then it is heated shortly and precisely, and the film contracts (VDI 3968-4, 2).

4.1.8 Mark

Before providing the container or loading unit for the next area, it is marked to be able to identify it and speed-up handling later on. For marking numbers, letters, labels, tags, symbols or colours can be used (ASTM D996, 7). Manufacturer, product, container global type, count, Universal Product Code (UPC) and Electronic Product Code (EPC) (Bowersox et al. 2010, 275-276) as well as ownership and destination (Brody and Marsh 1997, 536) are typical information provided during marking.

Usually, self-adhesive labels are used to attach this information to the loading unit (Drechsel and Vetter 2008, 167), but information can also be handwritten or printed directly on it (ASTM D996, 6). To stick on, the label has to be taken off, applied and pressed on (Bleisch 2003, 1211-1212).

Additionally, glue has to be applied if it is not a self-adhesive label. When printed at the workplace, it might be necessary to type the order number or press a button at a computer in order to confirm. The label contains one or more of the data items mentioned above (DIN EN 14943, 113). However, it might also be necessary to repeat these applying operations, because further or standardised information is needed. Hazardous material, for instance, requires an additional, special label. These labels are defined in ISO 780 and ISO 7000. If a label is used, we assume, as before, that supplies are provided.

4.1.9 Provide

The last sub-process is the provision of the shipping unit. It might be possible that the packer has to transport single or collected units to the next area, as among others Crostack and ten Hompel (2007, 41) describe. As mentioned before, however, it should be avoided that the packer has to leave his workplace.

Therefore, we assume that he takes the unit, with or without a device, and has to put it in an area out of his working space, which is marked as provision area for the next step. For this purpose, it might be required to do some steps, but it is not necessary to transport units over long distances, as the purpose is only to clear the workspace. Additionally, he needs to confirm that he has completed the packing job according to the requirements and returns to his workplace.

4.2 Information Flow

We already noticed in Section 4.1 that information is necessary to support the material flow. The task of the information system for logistic processes is to provide the right information at the right time and place (Martin 2009, 485). The information system provides all information details which are necessary to plan, operate and control the fulfilment of the customer order. Therefore, material and information flow need to be synchronised. The information flow can either be implemented with documents or with IT-systems (Crostack and ten Hompel 2007, 11). IT-systems are very common, one reason is the easier handling of a large variety of items, as Harsch and Wichmann (1990, 47) assessed for product packaging.

Information flows can be structured according to the same basic functions as the physical material flow, namely storing, transporting, processing and interpreting (Arnold and Furmans 2009, 329, cf. Section 4.1). Therefore, the tool of process chains can be chosen to show the information flow as well. We only consider the coordinating information flow, which is time-wise connected with the material flow (cf. Pielok 2010, 56). Consequently, the information usually accompanies the material and is relevant for the operative execution of the transport, transshipment and storing operations (Pfohl 2010, 73). For the packing process, this results in one information sub-process per packing process step. If we consider VDI 3590-1 (3) and the mandatory elements for picking, we can assume that the only information necessary for packing is the customer order. This is mandatory to be able to know where to send the unit, as all items of the order should already have been provided by the preceding process. Additionally, for automated systems information might be required like a database with master data of the items. Thus, in the following, we will describe the information related to each of the process steps introduced in Section 4.1.

While 'preparing the job' mainly information provided by the order is used. The information usually includes destination, article numbers, amount, weight and potentially special customer requirements. To receive this information, the order itself, a packing list, the delivery note or digital information are used. Thereby, the packing list and the delivery note have to be generated first. This usually happens in advance and we do not regard it as a part of the packing process. In order to get the digital information it might be necessary to identify the right job within a list of jobs, which can be done by scanning the job. At the same time, the packer confirms the start of the job and begins the processing. This could also be the signal towards the system to start printing jobs for labels and documents.

For 'preparing the packaging', and especially the decision on the packaging there are two possible approaches: either, the packer decides based on information about quantity and destination, or packaging material proposals are provided. To be able to continuously improve the proposals, sometimes these systems also need a feedback on which packaging was finally used, or at least if the packaging differs from the proposed one.

The sub-process 'packing' can be supported by the provision of a packing pattern. This step might also require a confirmation, or it has to be documented that the products where packed properly, e.g. by taking a photo. If 'checking' is required, all necessary parameters such as types, amounts, weights, etc. have to be provided and after checking they need to be confirmed.

In accordance to the packaging material proposal, there might also be a proposal or an instruction which protection material or securing method should be used for a given case. Again, it might be necessary to document or confirm the proper usage, in order to avoid liability claims.

If documents are necessary, they have to be provided or the information contained has to be available, so that they can be printed as required. The same applies for 'marking' or labelling of the unit. Not only information about the destination is expected, but it must also be indicated whether additional labels are necessary, for example to mark hazardous material. For both sub-processes it can be necessary to confirm or document the correct execution.

In case there are several provision areas, information where to 'provide' the unit has to be available. At the same time, usually a signal is given to indicate the end of the job and the availability of the packing workplace to start a new one. This information can also be used to inform the following process or the customer about the current status of the job.

4.3 Organisation

In Section 4.1, we focused on the material flow for packing. To be able to process jobs correctly, completely and in time, certain organisational and operational structures need to be in place as well. The organisational structure defines functions, tasks and authorities, whereas the operational structure defines the flow of data and information as well as the procedure of order processing (Gudehus 2010, 48).

4.3.1 Organisational Structure

Packing is characterised by a clear sequence structure and starts with the arrival of items for packing which are combined with the packaging to create a shipping unit (Dzeik 2008, 7). On the one hand, items for packing can be of different processing depth, e.g. articles without packaging, product packaged goods, small load carrier, parcels. On the other hand, shipping units can also be of different processing depth, e.g. messaging bags, small load carriers, packages, pallets. As mentioned in Section 2.1, it is sometimes necessary to link several packing processes before providing shipping units to the next area.

Traditionally, for packaging areas directly adjacent to production, there are three of these stages and as a result packing is described from primary to tertiary packing (cf. Section 2.2 and Schuster 1991, 256). DIN 55405 (7), in contrast, does not limit the number of stages in the packing process, but refers to primary packing as the starting stage and to packing of loading units as the final stage of the linked packing processes. In distribution centres, a single stage of packing might only be required, but it is also possible to have multiple stages. To give an example, it is very common to pack items into corrugated containers first and to pack these containers on a pallet in a next stage. Often, these stages are not combined at one packing workplace, but they take place at different ones. Still, these stages are performed one after the other. Even if it is the same packing workplace, it is also possible to analyse the stages separately and to link them later on to depict the whole process (Wisser 2009, 14 and Dzeik 2008, 33).

The individual stages resemble each other concerning the order and purpose of the sub-processes, even though the characteristics of the sub-processes differ. For instance to 'secure' a unit, in the first stage tape is used to secure the individual package, whereas in the second stage this and further packages are packed on a pallet and stretch film is used to secure it. The process chain illustrated in Figure 4.2 shows the typical material flow of the packing process. It is simply linked and executed several times, one time for each stage. In the next section, we will show how the sub-processes of one process chain can be arranged.

4.3.2 Operational Structure

As mentioned in Section 4.1, the packing process presented shows a typical order of how a job could be performed in a distribution centre. It could be organised in a different way as well, depending on the set-up. Still, there are some restrictions which we need to obey when performing the job.

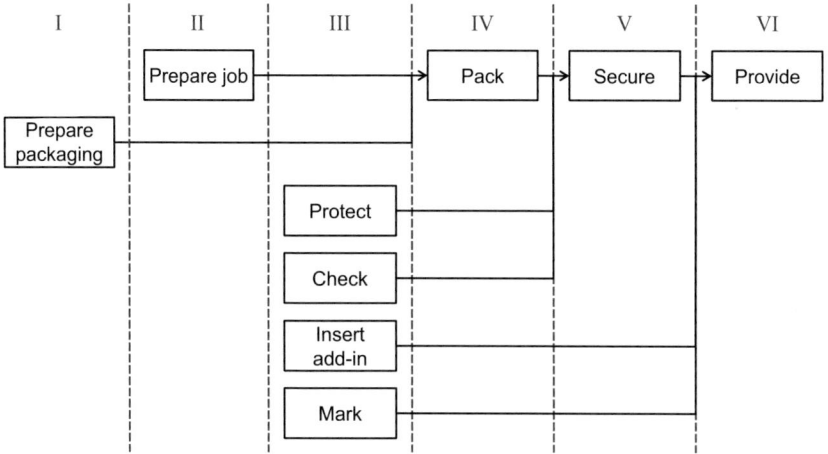

Figure 4.4: Precedence graph for the packing process

We have chosen a precedence graph in order to illustrate this operational order. The method of precedence graphs originates in assembly and is used to show operations and their relationship (Grote 2011, 100). Figure 4.4 indicates the precedence graph for the packing process. The sub-processes are shown as vertices and are listed according to their earliest possible execution (Westkämper 2006, 162). Their relation is shown using edges between them and the arrow indicates the latest possible execution. We identified the following dependencies between the packing sub-processes:

1. Prepare the packaging is the first possible step, as this sub-process is not even necessarily performed by the packer. It might already be performed earlier by another person or machine and pre-erected packages are provided to the packer. In any case, the sub-process

needs to be finished before the items can be packed into or onto the packaging.

2. Also preparing the job needs to be done at the beginning of the process, as unlike as for prepare packaging a job needs to be available. Further, information and decisions about required materials need to be provided for the following steps.

3. To protect the items, it might be necessary to insert cushioning material into the unit before items are packed, but the packaging needs to exist already. Due to accessibility, it has to be completed before the unit is secured.

4. The check of completeness is only possible if one knows what should be checked, hence after preparing the job. It can be done before packing items, but it needs to be finished before the shipping unit is secured, as access to the goods is limited afterwards.

5. Add-ins can be put into the shipping unit or outside onto it, but need to be placed there before provision. Information about add-ins need to be available, therefore 'insert add-in' is depicted after 'prepare job'.

6. The shipping unit can be marked as soon as the packaging is prepared and information is available, but has to be finished before the shipping unit is being provided to the next area, otherwise information might get lost.

7. The packing itself cannot be performed until it is clear how the items have to be processed and before the packaging has been prepared. It needs to be finished before the unit is secured.

8. The securing process needs to occur after the packing process, as the purpose is to protect these packed goods. Before providing the unit to the next area, securing has to be finished.

9. The provision to the next area has to be the last step and all subprocess have to be finished before, as otherwise information is lost or the job was not finished correctly.

After investigating the packing process in detail, we want to focus on how the sub-processes are influenced regarding time requirements in order to perform the activities necessary for each step.

5 Morphological Analysis

In Chapter 4, we described the material and information flow as well as the organisation of the packing process. In this Chapter, we want to identify parameters influencing the time needed for the packing process. For this purpose, we use a morphological analysis. The morphological method was introduced by Zwicky (1966) who used it first as a creativity technique to design new products. Later on, he also used it to structure relations for all kind of phenomena, activities and ideas, especially if the problem had numerous solutions (ibid., 48, 55). The aim of the method is to comprehensively research within a well-defined problem, and during this process, to consider all essential relations concerning the problem without prejudice (ibid., 42, 114). Therefore, the method is useful to analyse complex problems in an integral way (ibid., 164). Nowadays, the method is used to investigate relationships of multidimensional, non-quantifiable problems (Ritchey 2006, 792).

To apply this method in a structured way, the methodology of the morphological box (sometimes referred to as Zwicky box) is used (Zwicky 1966, 114). According to Zwicky (1966, 116-117), the following steps should be included in the analysis:

1. Exact definition and if necessary, generalization of a problem.

2. Determination of all influencing parameters.

3. Construction of the morphological box, including specifications of the parameters, which are exclusive from each other.

4. Analysis of the box, based on chosen criteria.

5. Decision on the solution and refining it.

The advantage of this methodology is that an overview of the solution space is given, which eases the discussion about possible solutions (Meier 2005, 108).

In this thesis, we want to use morphological analysis in order to reveal influences on the packing time and identify important parameters. This separation of generating alternatives and assessing them (Hauschildt and Salomo 2011, 292) is also reflected in the following sections: first, we give an exact definition of the problem, before we identify influencing parameters, and construct morphological boxes for each process step. In the next step, we asses these boxes, and finally reduce them to one condensed box including the most relevant parameters. Based on this, we derive assumptions for the cycle time.

5.1 Definition of the Problem

In order to perform morphological analysis, we need to formulate the research question: Which parameters influence packing time in distribution centres independently from the respective order, and which specifications need to be distinguished, in order to be able to calculate the time required?

Performing the analysis and knowing the parameters as well as their specifications shall allow us to:

- Reveal which parameters are significant concerning the packing time and need to stay in focus while formulating the cycle time.

- Identify commonalities between parameters.

- Decide how they should be taken into account for the mathematical formulation.

These results are summarised in Section 5.4.

5.2 Determination of Influencing Parameters

In this section, we want to identify possible parameters influencing packing time. In order to keep an overview, a morphological box for each process step, which we identified in Chapter 4.1, is used, as one box should only contain between six and eight parameters (cf. Gassmann and Sutter 2008, 308). In order to illustrate the options, we state a question to describe parameters and we explain possible specifications and why they are distinguished. Further, we show the resulting morphological box, in which we sort the specifications according to the anticipated effort, where possible.

Some of the influencing parameters are mainly relevant for manual implementations, but as we try to get a full overview, they have been integrated in this first step. Other parameters influence packing, such as the number of articles per order or the sample size, but later on in the calculation they will be integrated as a coefficient in the mathematical formulation (cf. n in Formula 6.2) and they cannot be influenced while planning, because the customer order is a given. This is why they are not listed in the box. We include other parameters in the analysis, which will be most likely modelled as coefficients as well, but in most cases they are related to the packing system, such as distances, and not to the customer order.

For information related process steps, as well as for transport, the specifications 'automated' and 'not required' are usually grouped. This is because no manpower is required for automated activities, and while the automated system processes information or transports an unit the packer is able to perform another step.

The following sections are structured as mentioned above, and we investigate each process step identified in Section 4.1.

5.2.1 Prepare Job

Time to prepare the next job mainly depends on the necessary activities, and on how they are performed. An overview of the influencing parameters and the specifications is given in the morphological box shown in Table 5.1. We describe the parameters and their specifications in the following.

Item handling	one hand	both hands	moving required	
			no device	device
Item weight	< 1kg	1kg - 8kg	8kg - 22kg	> 22kg
Choose job	automated/ not required	pick randomly	priority	specified job
Confirmation on start	automated/ not required	manual/ automated	manual input	manual
Identification	automated/ not required	manual/ automated	manual comparison	
Transport of items to workplace	automated/ not required	semi-automated	manual	
			no device	device
	several items with one transport	single items		
Decision on packaging	provided proposal	standard	packer's decision	
Decision on protection material	not required	provided proposal	standard	packer's decision
Decision on securing method	provided proposal	standard	packer's decision	

Table 5.1: Morphological box for 'prepare job'

How are items handled? Items vary a lot considering dimensions, and size of items is regarded as influencing parameter by several authors (Bleisch et al. 2011, 32, Martin 2009, 74, Dzeik 2008, 9, 118, Hellström and Saghir 2007, 203, 206, Gudehus 1973, 47, VDI 3590-1, VDI 3612). Lee and Lye (2003, 172-174) additionally distinguish the required effort of grasping and rotational symmetry of the item as parameters. Rotational symmetry is more important for product packaging because the item needs to fit into a specially designed packaging with low tolerance. However, for manual packing, it is mainly important how the item can be handled, as activities

5.2 Determination of Influencing Parameters

necessary to accomplish a sub-process are connected with it. If the item is small, it might be handled using one hand and if it is bigger, both hands are required. For pallets, for instance, it is even necessary that the packer moves, as the size of the pallet is bigger than the space within his reach (cf. Figure 5.1). Additionally, it can be necessary to use a helping device.

How heavy are items that need to be handled? Mainly for the manual process weight is important, as it is easier to handle lighter items. MTM methodology distinguishes between items lighter than 1 kg, between 1 and 8 kg and between 8 and 22 kg (MTM 2012b). As we want to consider the packing of large load carriers as well, which often happens using devices, items can also be heavier than 22 kg.

How is the next job chosen? In some cases it is not necessary to decide which job has to be taken next in the packing area, as only one job at a time is provided for packing, and decision on it has been made beforehand. In other cases, it does not matter which one is taken, as all orders have the same priority, and need to be finished e.g. at the end of the day, so the packer just picks the nearest one, for example. On the other hand, there might be priorities, for example when having express orders or if cut-off times have to be met. In this case perhaps, two different supply areas have to be checked for packing jobs or priority signals have to be obeyed. The case in which the packer needs to pick a specific job according to a printed list or by following commands of an IT-system might consume the most time, because he has to search for this specific one out of several provided packing jobs.

How is the confirmation about starting the job given? For some systems it might not be necessary to confirm the start of the packing job at all. This might be, because the job had been scanned automatically and information had been processed within the IT-System. Another possibility is that the signal is just not necessary or given later when the job is finished. In other cases, the job is scanned manually, and information is processed automatically using a bar code, which is less time consuming than for example the entering of an order number into the IT-system manually, or confirming it manually by writing into a list and/or setting a signal. Barthel in Yam (2010, 294) confirms this, and additionally argues that the error rate is lower when scanning is employed.

How is the job identified? In order to decide on some options for packing, like the type of protection material that shall be used, it is necessary to identify the job. Information might be accumulated in an IT-system which displays information automatically. In other systems, it is necessary to scan the job, or a unit out of it, manually first, to be able to get the appropriate information displayed. It is the most time consuming when comparing the order number from a packing list with the order number provided on the picked items, for instance.

Is a transport necessary between the point of provision and the packing workplace, or is there a distance between the point of provision and the packing workplace which needs to be covered by the packing resource? As mentioned before, the packer should not leave the packing workplace, for example, to pick the packing job. So the best set-up is that in which transporting is not required, because packing jobs are provided directly at the packing workplace. Therefore, the provision is automated, or another person, not related to the resource of the packing workplace, provides the jobs. For semi-automated transport, the packer can use a device, like a pallet truck, which he needs to conduct, but he does not have to move himself. Manual transport requires a movement of the packer. He might have a manual platform truck or a pallet jack to help him transporting the items. Another possibility is that items are transported manually, without a device, but they might be consolidated in a box, for example. Following VDI 3590-1 (6), the time to get a hold on the item(s) to be transported should be included in the transport time.

As mentioned, more than one item at a time can be transported as well. This can be the case, for instance, if a trolley is used for picking, and several items and/or orders are combined on it. In other cases, like for pallet transport, it might not be possible to transport more than one item or order at a time, so they need to be transported separately.

How is a decision made which packaging should be used for the job? One possibility is that a proposal is provided with the packing list or within the IT-System and has been calculated beforehand based on the order and master data on the products. This usually also applies if the system is highly automated. Another option is that standards have been defined, and the packer has to choose among these. An example for a standard would be that the packer has to choose a specific kind of corrugated

5.2 Determination of Influencing Parameters 57

container if the orders weight is more than 20 kg. In other cases, the packer decides on packaging, which tends to take longer as he has to consider items dimensions, quantities, fragility, destination, etc. depending on the assortment. But also in this last case, one could use guidelines which provide criteria to decide on packaging, protection and securing, like for example in VDI 3968-1 and ten Hompel et al. (2007, 46).

How is a decision made which protection material should be used for the job? For protection material the same options apply as for the packaging, but as cushioning material might not be necessary an additional option must be that cushioning material is not required at all. This is often the case if pallets are packed or if items have no sharp edges so that they cannot damage each other.

How is a decision made which securing method should be applied for the job? A decision on the securing method is also necessary, and again the same options are possible as for the packaging material. Either the decision is made beforehand, or there is a standard stating that whenever the shipping container exceeds 20kg, the corrugated container has to be additionally strapped, or the packer needs to decide according to items requirements. Decision criteria to consider are provided e.g. in ten Hompel et al. (2007, 47).

5.2.2 Prepare Packaging

Apart from the activities and their realisation, the time to prepare the packaging is influenced by the dimensions and weight of the packaging. Table 5.2 gives an overview and its aspects are discussed in the following.

How is the packaging handled? Packaging material as well varies a lot with regard to dimensions and weight. Therefore, we distinguish the same specifications as we have previously done for items in Section 5.2.1. Necessary operations for manual systems vary, for automated systems it does not depend so much on the dimensions as the activity does not change, whereas the size of the machine will vary and the time to perform the activity.

Packaging handling	one hand	both hands	moving required		
			no device	device	
Packaging weight	< 1kg	1kg - 8kg	8kg - 22kg	> 22kg	
Packaging material provision	in reach	out of reach			
Positioning of packaging	not required	automated	manual		
Set up packaging	not required	automated	semi-automated	manual	
	one side	two sides	four sides		
Fix joints	not required	automated	semi-automated	manual	
	lock	glue	tape	stitch	
Open packaging	not required	automated	manual		
Assemble loading unit	not required	semi-automated	manual		

Table 5.2: Morphological box for 'prepare packaging'

How heavy is packaging that needs to be handled? For the packaging we also distinguish between the different specifications of weight, as these categories are generally used with identical specifications.

Where is the packaging material provided? For the manual process step it is important where the material, which the packer has to take to prepare the packaging, is located. It might be in reach on a shelf containing corrugated containers for example, or out of the space within reach, and he has to move to get a pallet for instance. Here, naturally the activities vary depending on the case. The space within reach in Figure 5.1 refers to the physiologically maximal possible space, which is ten percent smaller than the anatomically possible space within reach (Bullinger 1994, 205).

5.2 Determination of Influencing Parameters

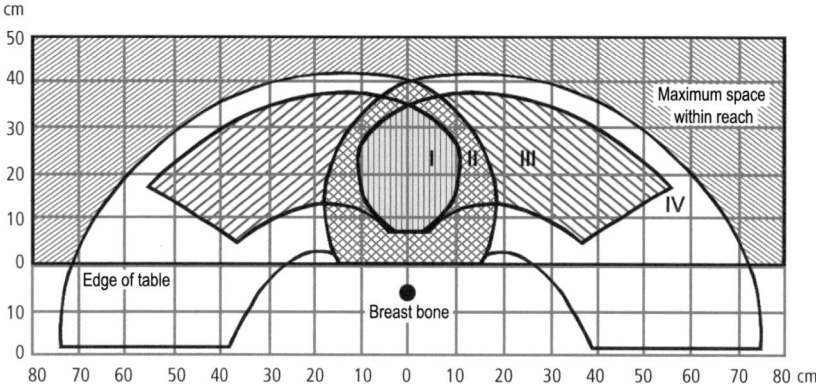

Figure 5.1: Working zones for different activities (following Bokranz and Landau 2006, 280)

Which activities have to be performed and how are they performed? As mentioned in Chapter 4, activities performed within a sub-process can vary. With regard to time necessary to perform them, it is not only required to know if they are performed at all, but also how they are performed. For the activities of positioning, setting up, fixing joints and opening the first option is that they are not required. The second and third options are automated and manual systems. For setting up and fixing joints, it is additionally possible to use aids to speed up the manual process. ASTM D1974 (3) mentions hand-held and table top dispensers as the most common equipment to aid fixing the joint. Therefore, we also distinguish the specification of 'semi-automated'. Other activities, like fixing a corrugated container on a pallet, are referred to as 'assemble loading unit', and we differentiate between not required, semi-automated and manual activities. We do not differentiate automated as this activity is so specific that it is hard to completely automate it.

For setting up the packaging it is further relevant, how many lids of a corrugated container need to be closed, for instance. We distinguish the specifications: one side, two sides and four sides. This is relevant especially for the manual process, as with box erecting machines activities could be parallelised (for details see Bleisch 2003, 339).

The activities necessary for fixing joints depend on the method used (Dzeik 2008, 118), so we distinguish locking of a container, glueing, taping and stitching.

5.2.3 Pack

Packing items also does not only depend on the activities, and how they are performed, but also on the characteristics of items and packaging. An overview of parameters and their specification is given in Table 5.3.

Packaging handling	one hand	both hands	moving required	
			no device	device
Item handling	one hand	both hands	moving required	
			no device	device
	several items with one grasp	single items		
	automated	semi-automated	manual	
Item weight	< 1kg	1kg - 8kg	8kg - 22kg	> 22kg
Type of items	identical units	modular units	variety	
Item stability	dimensionally stable	flexible	fragile	
Order of items	not relevant	according to packing requirements	chaotic	
Positioning items	not required	packer's decision	standard	provided proposal

Table 5.3: Morphological box for 'pack'

How is the packaging handled? Same as for preparing the packaging, dimensions of the packaging influence the packing process. Therefore, we

5.2 Determination of Influencing Parameters

can distinguish the same cases for packaging handling as before: one hand, both hands, moving with or without device.

How are items handled? As for preparing the job, we can apply the following specifications: if one hand, both hands, or a movement (with or without device) is required. Further, it makes a difference if items have to be grasped separately or if several can be handled together (Gudehus 1973, 47).

Additionally, the technical implementation is important for item handling: packing might be automated with a robot grasping items, semi-automated if the packer uses a device to grasp or lift items, or completely manual. Automated systems are rarely used, because even high technical and financial efforts still result in a low output (Bleisch 2003, 415). For packing into containers Günthner and Lammer (2009, 75) amend, that using a robot is only reasonable if items are already grasped or if there is another mechanism to get items into the container, e.g. by a chute. Automating pallet packing is more common and different methods exist, but usually the boxes to be packed should have the same size (cf. Bleisch et al. 2011, 452).

How heavy are items that need to be handled? As for preparing the job, also for packing the weight of items needs to be considered (Bleisch et al. 2011, 32, Hellström and Saghir 2007, 206, Gudehus 1973, 47, VDI 3590-1, VDI 3612). This is particularly the case as during packing usually every item has to be moved. Again, we distinguish between items lighter than 1 kg, between 1 and 8 kg, between 8 and 22 kg, and heavier than 22 kg.

Are items differing in size and shape? Reusable packaging like plastic boxes are usually dimensioned in a modular way. Often, the modularity is connected to the pallet size as well, and companies start to adapt this modular sizing for their corrugated packaging to ease handling (one example is the company Adolf Würth GmbH & Co. KG). Modularity positively influences the time to build the unit (Martin 2009, 74). It is easier for the packer to decide where to put the unit, as well as it is easier for the automated system to calculate the packing pattern and position it properly. Of course, the task is even easier if all items are identical, but this is usually not the case for packing in distribution centres. If items vary, more time is required because it might even be necessary to reposition them and therefore grasp and move them once more.

How stable are items and how do they have to be treated therefore? Another influence on the time necessary for packing is the stability of items (Hellström and Saghir 2007, 203, 206, VDI 3590-2, 2). According to Bleisch (2003, 440) and Dietz and Lippmann (1986, 15), we distinguish between dimensionally stable, flexible and fragile items. Stable items are easier to handle, because movement can be anticipated easier. Movement of flexible items is harder to anticipate, on the other hand it might be easier to pack them together. For instance clothes wrapped in a plastic film are easier packed than boxes. Fragile items need to be handled with care and might not be stackable either, so extra time is necessary to pack them (cf. Gudehus 1973, 47). We do not consider different kinds of sensitivity of items here, as sensitivity mainly influences the decision on packaging (Großmann and Kaßmann 2007, 36), but not the time needed to pack.

Are items in proper order to pack them? If items are very robust and/or identical, it does not matter in which order they are packed into a corrugated container or onto a pallet. But it could also be necessary to put heavier items onto the bottom of the unit, for example. This has an effect on the packing time, and we distinguish if the items are already ordered, for instance according to weight, or if they are provided chaotically, and the packer or the machine has to put them into the right order, before packing them.

How are items positioned? The packer can decide where to position items while packing, but here as well a standard or a proposal can be provided, as we have seen in Section 5.2.1 for the decision about packaging, protecting and securing material. This time, besides the intellectual a physical activity is required as well. Therefore, positioning can consume more time if the packer has to study a packing pattern first, before he can place items on a specific position, or if he has to arrange items according to a standard. Otherwise, it also can ease work for him, because in that case trial and error is not necessary. A packing standard is described in Gudehus and Kotzab (2012, 342) as general packing rules for the sequence, orientation and stacking of units, whereas the proposal is referred to as packing scheme which is calculated for each unit separately. Both usually already consider packing restrictions such as stacking or safety restrictions (cf. Gudehus and Kotzab 2012, 342), which otherwise need to be considered by the packer.

5.2.4 Check

The main reason for checking within the packing area is to have satisfied customers. Customers do not want to receive wrong items or an incorrect amount of items, especially if the lead time between order and delivery is long. Apart from the sample size, which needs to be modelled as factor in calculations, checking is mainly influenced by which parameters are checked, and how this is realised. For the receiving area the following checks are listed in VDI 3612: identity check, counting, weighing, measuring and quality inspection. We assume counting and weighing are possible specifications of checking the correct quantity, whereas measuring is a specification of a quality check. Further, we also consider a volume check. Apart from the type, handling size has an influence on the time needed for checking. An overview is given in Table 5.4.

Item handling	one hand	both hands	moving required	
			no device	device
Item weight	< 1kg	1kg - 8kg	8kg - 22kg	> 22kg
Amount check	not required	automated	manual weighing	counting
Identity check	not required	automated	manual/ automated	manual comparison
Volume check	not required	automated	semi-automated	manual
Quality inspection	not required	automated	semi-automated	manual
	condition product packing	completeness check product	measuring	functional
Confirmation	automated	manual/ automated	manual input	manual
	per order	per position	per unit	

Table 5.4: Morphological box for 'check'

How are items handled? Checking of items also depends on their size, as they might have to be moved in order to read the identification number, for example. So the same criteria as for packing apply (cf. Section 5.2.3).

How heavy are items that need to be handled? While checking items they might have to be moved, in order to be able to check their article code, for instance. Therefore, it can be necessary to lift them and as a consequence weight influences the process as well. We chose the same specifications as for packing (cf. Section 5.2.3).

How is the amount of items checked? In order to have satisfied customers, often the right amount of picked items is double-checked at the packing workplace, after checking it while picking. This step can be automated, for example the box including the picked items is weighted before items are packed. In this case, in order to be effective master data needs to be accurate, and mistakes are not necessarily discovered, as the weight of different items can be very similar (Crostack et al. 2007, 46). Weighing is also used as a manual method, which consumes more time, as the packer needs to grasp items, put them on the scale and might even need to grasp them again. Another option is counting the items which is also performed by the packer.

How is the identity of items checked? To satisfy the customer, apart from the amount of items, the identity can be checked as well. This might be a more automated step, if the items are scanned during their transportation to the packing area, or it might be partly manually because the packer has to scan the item, and only the information is processed automatically. Another option is that the packer has to compare the item numbers with the packing list, for example (Crostack et al. 2007, 46). This usually takes longer, because he has to process the information as well.

How is the volume check executed? Especially for pallets which are sent to an automated high bay storage within one of the next steps in the supply-chain, it might be necessary to perform a volume check as well. This could be done automatically with sensors, when the pallet is automatically transported to the next area, for example. But it might also be possible that the packer needs to transport the pallet through a sensor gate, where dimensions are measured. Last but not least, it is also possible that the packer himself measures the dimensions of the items or unit.

5.2 Determination of Influencing Parameters

How is the quality inspected? In most of the distribution centres there is no quality inspection while packing as this is usually already performed in an earlier stage, for example within the receiving area. Of course, the level of automation might be different for quality inspection as well, which effects the time necessary to perform the check.

On the other hand, the time needed also depends on what kind of check has to be performed: often it is only a visual inspection of the packaging (Crostack et al. 2007, 46), because the customer likes to have a product packaging without scratches and with intact edges, as he then assumes that there are no transport damages. In other cases, the packer checks that the product packaging contains all parts, and consequently has to open the primary packaging, which consumes a lot of time. Further, it might be necessary to measure if certain nominal values are met (Crostack et al. 2007, 46), or even the function of the products can be checked.

This last case is very specific and not a task of logistic. It is therefore a separate area of research and as a result we list it in the morphological box (cf. Table 5.4), but do not enquire it further.

How is the check confirmed? The information that either the check was successful or that rework has to be done is usually processed automatically for automated systems. In other cases, it is a mixture as a bar code has to be scanned manually and information is processed automatically, or the packer needs to take a photo which is processed automatically. Further, it can be necessary to enter information manually into a computer system, or to sign or check the successful checking in a list (following VDI 3590-1, 5).

This activities can be performed once for the whole order, per order position on the packing list, or for each single item (VDI 3590-1, 5).

5.2.5 Protect

The choice on which protection material can be used and what methods are applied depend on many parameters. We do not want to discuss this here in detail, as the general choice is usually made beforehand, and we already considered time for the packer to decide whether to use one of his choices or not within the preparing time. Activities that need to be performed within this sub-process depend on which kind of material is used, on the size of and access to the packaging, as well as the implementation and the provision of material. The influencing parameters and their specification are shown in Table 5.5.

Unit handling	one hand	both hands	moving required		
			no device	device	
Access to unit	five sides	four sides	three sides	two sides	one side
Protection material handling	automated	semi-automated	manual		
Protection material provision	in reach	out of reach			
Type of protection material	loose/ liquid material	piece material	yard material		

Table 5.5: Morphological box for 'protect'

How can the unit be handled? As in previous steps, the packaging has to be handled for protection. This time, the packaging includes all the items, and is therefore referred to as unit. Specifications are the same as before.

Where is it possible to access the unit? To insert protection material it is necessary to access the packed unit, hence we differentiate between how many sides can be used for this purpose, according to Section 5.2.2.

How is it realised technically? The time for protecting depends on the technical implementation. The used material might be inserted or applied automatically, it might be possible that the packer uses a device, or that he inserts protection material manually.

Where is the protection material provided? Another parameter influencing the time is the position of the material supply, especially for the manual process. If the packer just needs to reach for it, or if he has to move, in order to handle or to get it.

What kind of material is used to protect the unit? As mentioned before, activities that consume time mainly depend on the material being used (Dzeik 2008, 118). For protection, loose material like chips, liquid foam packaging or glue needs to be applied, covering the surface of the units. Piece material, like any kind of cushions or the securing layers for pallets, are repetitively packed inside the unit along with the items until the shipping unit is filled. Also yard material, like paper or different kind of air cushion films, can be used. They are usually provided on larger rolls and need to be cut and partly even crumpled in order to pack them into the shipping unit. As the different types of protection material should exclude one another, they can be considered as one influencing parameter, and we do not need to list activities.

5.2.6 Insert Add-in

There are different materials that can be added to the order, as mentioned in Chapter 4.1. The range starts with sheets of paper and continues all the way to bigger things, like advertising gifts or catalogues. Time needed to pack them also depends on their number, the handling as well as on the required activities. Table 5.6 gives an overview.

How are add-ins handled? As mentioned before, additional material can vary, and it is necessary to know how it is handled, in order to determine the time needed. Same as for the other process steps, we differentiate between the use of one or two hands and whether moving is required.

In most of the cases, add-ins are inserted manually, but it is also possible to do it semi-automatically if the packer uses a device or to have it automated by dropping add-ins into the container while being on a conveyor, or by using a robot.

If there are several documents, there is a possibility that these all are papers, and that they can be handled together. But in other cases, separate handling can be necessary, as add-ins differ or cannot be handled together.

Add-in handling	one hand	both hands	moving required	
			no device	device
	automated	semi-automated	manual	
	handled as one	handled separately		
Add-in provision	in reach	out of reach		
Add-in position	inside the unit	outside on the unit		
Initialisation print	automated/ not required	manual/ automated	manual input	
Fold	not required	automated	semi-automated	manual
Inserting bag	not required	automated	semi-automated	manual

Table 5.6: Morphological box for 'insert add-in'

Where are add-ins provided? As before, the location for the provision of add-ins has an influence on time required to insert: either the packer just needs to reach for them, or he needs to move in order to get hold on them.

Where are add-ins positioned? Documents might be either inserted into the unit, or they need to be attached to the unit from outside. Other items like catalogues are usually inserted. As the position needs to be more precise for add-ins attached outside, 'outside of the unit' is regarded as more time consuming. Additionally, it usually is necessary to insert them into a bag to protect them from stresses during transport.

Does printing need to be initialised? Documents might already be printed and are just provided, or printing might be started automatically when the job is started. In other cases, it might be necessary to scan a code manually, or even a manual input might be necessary to initialise the printing process.

5.2 Determination of Influencing Parameters

Are documents folded? Are documents inserted into an envelope or a bag?
Packing lists or invoices are often folded, and inserted into an envelope. Naturally, both activities might occur also as a single activity and the activities can be automated, the packer might use a device to speed up the operation or just perform it completely manual.

5.2.7 Secure

The time to secure a unit depends mainly on the size of the unit, and the activities that need to be performed. An overview is given in Table 5.7.

Unit handling	one hand	both hands	moving required	
			no device	device
Unit weight	< 1kg	1kg - 8kg	8kg - 22kg	> 22kg
Securing material provision	in reach	out of reach		
Working area	decentralised at workplace	central area		
Close package	not required	automated	semi-automated	manual
	one side	two sides	four sides	
Fix joints	not required	automated	semi-automated	manual
	lock	glue	tape	stitch
Strap unit	not required	automated	semi-automated	manual
Stretch wrap unit	not required	automated	semi-automated	manual
Shrink wrap unit	not required	automated	semi-automated	

Table 5.7: Morphological box for 'secure'

How is the unit handled? For securing, time needed depends a lot on the dimensions of the unit (Martin 2009, 74, Großmann and Kaßmann 2007,

24). Therefore, we differentiate again if it is possible to handle it with one or both hands, or if it is necessary for the packer to move, and whether a device is needed.

How heavy are units that need to be handled? Not only the dimensions are important, but also the weight as units might need to be turned in order to secure them (cf. Großmann and Kaßmann 2007, 24). The classification is according to item weights for preparing the job (cf. Section 5.2.1).

Where is securing material provided? It is also important to know where the securing material is provided. Is it in reach or out of reach.

Where are devices located? Packing work-areas are designed differently compared to each other regarding layout. Of course, to minimise packing time it is best if the packer stays on his decentralised workplace, and does not have to leave this place to transport units. However, often it is necessary to share devices, as they are expensive, and these devices are located in a common area for several or all packers. Consequently, the packer has to leave the workplace, and transport the unit in order to secure it, for example.

Is the unit closed? And where? Units, like corrugated containers, bins or crates, usually have to be closed. This operation is accomplished either automatically, when units are conveyed through a device and thereby closed, it can be done semi-automatically, where units need to be pushed by the packer through a device, but lids are closed automatically, or completely manually.

Another influencing parameter is how many lids need to be closed. It might be only on one side or one lid, but it is very common that one has to close two or even four sides of the unit.

Is it necessary to fix the joint? How are they fixed? Following FEFCO (2007), it might not be necessary to fix the joint of the lids, as they can be self-adhesive. Otherwise, the process can be automated with a closing machine (cf. DIN EN 415-1, 10) or semi-automated. Here, the packer has to push the unit through a device usually. The last alternative is that it has to be done completely in a manual way.

But this is not the only difference in time necessary to fix joints. It also depends on the method used to fix them. The lids of crates or bins are

5.2 Determination of Influencing Parameters

often only locked, whereas corrugated containers are usually glued or taped. Glueing is often used in combination with automated systems, whereas taping is typically used if manually fixing the joints. Another way to fix the joints in different degrees of automation is to use stitches.

Is the unit strapped, stretched and/or shrink wrapped? How is it done? As described in Section 4.1, these three methods are the most commonly used ones for securing, and combine different necessary activities. Therefore, they are distinguished in order to be able to calculate time consumption.

Another influencing parameter is the degree of automation. For all methods there are various automated and semi-automated solutions, which are described for example by Ebeling (1990, 78). If a system is semi-automated, the packer might be supported by a small vehicle fetching the strap under the pallet so that he does not need to kneel. For stretching he can be supported by a rotating disc and eventually also a film carriage (cf. Großmann and Kaßmann 2007, 32), so that he does not need to walk around the pallet. For strapping and stretching it is possible to do this completely manually, but for shrink wrapping a device is necessary in any case as the film needs to be heated (cf. VDI 3968-5, 21). We sort the specifications automated, semi-automated, manual in the given order, because for example VDI 3968-5 (9-13) indicates the following throughputs for stretch wrapping with the respective degree of automation: automated 120 pallets/h, semi-automated 20 pallets/h and manual 20-50 pallets/day.

5.2.8 Mark

The time for marking is influenced by the way marking is performed, as well as the question where the material is stored. Table 5.8 gives an overview of the influencing parameters.

Where is the material needed for marking provided? Again, it is important to know where the material is provided, as it influences the total time of packing when the packer needs to leave the packing workplace, or if the machine needs to wait until material is provided.

How is printing initialised? If a label is needed, it might be necessary to initialise printing if this is neither implemented in an automated manner

Marking material provision	in reach	out of reach		
Initialisation print	automated/ not required	manual/ automated	manual input	
Mark	automated	semi-automated	manual	
	printed	self adhesive	glue	write

Table 5.8: Morphological box for 'mark'

nor required. It can be necessary to scan a bar code manually or to give a manual input.

How is marking realised technically? Which activities are necessary? For marking as well there are machines, like labelling machines, which can attach labels automatically. Details are described in DIN EN 415-1 (11). But there are also semi-automated machines, like a machine that removes the label, so that the packer only needs to attach it on the shipping unit. Naturally, it is also possible to do it completely manually.

Apart from the technical implementation, the time for marking depends on the activities (Dzeik 2008, 118). Activities necessary to mark a shipping unit can vary, and exclude one another. Sometimes, especially if the process is automated, marks are just directly printed on the unit. Another common case is to use self adhesive labels with the required information, which are removed from the paper and attached to the shipping unit. But it might also be possible that the packer has to glue a piece of paper or something else on the shipping unit, or that he needs to handwrite information on it.

5.2.9 Provide

Providing the packed shipping unit not only depends on the size and weight of the unit, but also on what kind of activities are necessary, as well as on how they are performed. An overview is given in Table 5.9.

5.2 Determination of Influencing Parameters

Unit handling	one hand	both hands	moving required	
			no device	device
Unit weight	< 1kg	1kg - 8kg	8kg - 22kg	> 22kg
Confirmation on end	automated/ not required	manual/ automated	manual input	manual
Clear workspace	automated	semi-automated	manual	
	push	put	bend	
Transport of units to provision area	automated/ not required	semi-automated	manual	
			no device	device
	several units with one transport	single units		

Table 5.9: Morphological box for 'provide'

How are units handled? Also for provision, it is necessary to know how units can be handled to be able to calculate the respective working time. Specifications are according to the previous sub-processes: one or both hands, moving with or without device.

How heavy are units? As shipping units need to be moved somehow in order to clear the workplace, also the weight of the units is relevant, at least if the process is manual. Again we differentiate between the categories analogue to MTM (2012b).

How is finishing a job confirmed? It might not be necessary to confirm the end of processing a job at all. Alternatively, again a mixture between manual and automated confirmation is possible by using a scanner, or confirmation is given by manually writing into a list and/or by manually setting a signal.

How is the workplace cleared up? Which activities are necessary to do so? It might not be necessary to provide the shipping unit actively, if the packer packs directly on a conveying system and after confirming the end of the job the unit is conveyed automatically, for example. A complete automation with a robot is possible for clearing as well. In semi-automated systems, the packer can use for instance a device to lift the unit. The last specification is that the packer needs to provide the shipping unit completely manually.

The least time consuming way to empty a workplace manually is to push the shipping unit on a conveyor. In other cases, the unit is grasped, lifted and put somewhere, for example onto a trolley. Sometimes, the packer has to bend additionally, because the conveyor is lower than the workplace and as bending consumes time we need to differentiate this as well.

How are units transported? Often shipping units need to be transported to provide them for the next process. Especially for small load carriers conveyors are used which means that the transport is automated. In other cases transport is semi-automated, for example when providing pallets using a pallet truck. Also manual means of transportation are possible, where the packer has to walk the distance. We have to further distinguish if he uses a device, like a trolley or a pallet jack, or not (following VDI 3590-1, 6).

Also here, time consumption depends on the set-up: whether several units are transported together, for example by putting them on a common trolley after packing, or if each unit is transported separately, which is necessary for pallets for instance.

5.3 Analysis of the Morphological Boxes

In this section, we want to analyse the parameters identified in the previous sections. As the nine morphological boxes result in $9.7 \cdot 10^{37}$ possible combinations, it is necessary to determine the importance of the parameters, and to refine them, in order to create one results box for the whole packing process in Section 5.4. This box will help us to identify important parameters, which we need to consider when deriving cycle time formulas in Chapter 6.

Meier (2005, 111) mentions four strategies in order to reduce the parameters:

5.3 Analysis of the Morphological Boxes

1. Use of reduction strategies.
2. Matrix of compatibility.
3. Alternating combination and selection.
4. Substitute solutions.

For the first strategy, the following process is recommended (Meier 2005, 111):

- Sort parameters according to their relevance.
- Defer parameters of low importance.
- Defer specifications which are not so useful.
- Combine specifications to categories.

We want to use this first strategy 'use of reduction strategies' and start by determining the relevance of parameters. In order to do this, we decided to perform an analysis of variance described in Section 5.3.3. Further, we want to seek to reduce the complexity of the problem by applying the other steps of the first strategy. We discuss results in Section 5.4.

The second strategy 'matrix of compatibility' compares all elements pairwise regarding their compatibility. We performed this analysis with a first draft of morphological boxes (cf. Weiblen and Breiner 2012, 202-203), but discovered that it does not help to reduce complexity, as almost all combinations are possible for packing.

Within the third strategy 'alternating combination and selection' a tree of possible solutions is created. As soon as a combination of parameters is not possible, the branch is not further regarded and marked. This results in a reduced number of possible branches. But here as well, we are confronted with the problem that parameters can be easily combined for packing, and only a few of the branches are not possible and can be reduced (cf. Weiblen and Breiner 2012, 203).

The last strategy, suggested by Meier (2005, 111) in order to reduce complexity, is to find substitute solutions. This analysis focuses on promising solutions as so called 'substitute solutions' first, whereas the other solutions are put aside and regarded later on. But in our case, where we want to find out which parameters should be focused on, and do not want to investigate further based on our assumptions, this possibility is not relevant.

Accordingly, we want to use the first strategy 'use of reduction strategies' and perform an analysis of variance in order to determine the effect of the influencing parameters on the packing time (cf. Dzeik and Picker 2003, 70). With this result, the morphological boxes can be reduced, and we can use the discovered insight to determine cycle times. To determine the effect of the influencing parameters, the extremes, in this case the ones with highest and lowest anticipated impact on duration, are modelled quantitatively using a predetermined motion time system. Consequently, the first section of this sub-chapter is on predetermined motion time systems, and the second one on the analysis of variance. The third section shows the results of the analysis for the morphological boxes identified in Section 5.2, and based on these presents a condensed morphological box. Implications for the cycle times are derived in this section as well.

5.3.1 Predetermined Motion Time Systems

We want to use the analysis of variance to derive which parameters need to be considered for the general cycle time formulas. Therefore, we also have to take a look at general times for processes. General times cannot be easily determined by measuring times of specific systems, as all influencing parameters have to be considered (REFA 1997, 10), instead one can use predetermined motion time systems to describe a system, even without observing an existing process (ten Hompel et al. 2011, 136, Heinz and Olbrich 1989, 20, John 1987, 15-16, 267 and Maynard et al. 1948, 17-18, 163-164). This is due to the fact that standard durations have been determined by analysing times in several different systems, and describing them with the help of boundary conditions and influencing parameters (Maynard et al. 1948, 29-30).

Different kinds of predetermined motion time systems have been developed. The most common ones are MTM (Methods Time Measurement), Work-Factor and the MOST-Technique (Maynard Operation Sequence Technique) (Crostack et al. 2007, 48-49, Heinz and Olbrich 1989, 14). According to Sautter et al. (1998, 47) (cf. Figure 5.2), MTM is the most popular regarding application (share of 50%) and level of awareness (share of 80%),

5.3 Analysis of the Morphological Boxes

and considers also qualitative influencing parameters (Heinz and Olbrich 1989, 14, 16). In a study of Sautter et al. (1998, 53) the participants indicated the possibility to use MTM for the design of workplaces as advantage. Another advantage of MTM is that over the years further systems derived from the basic MTM system, where eight basic motions of hands and arms as well as two eye functions and nine movements are regarded (Bokranz and Landau 2006, 508-509), have been developed and can be used additively (Sautter et al. 1998, 53).

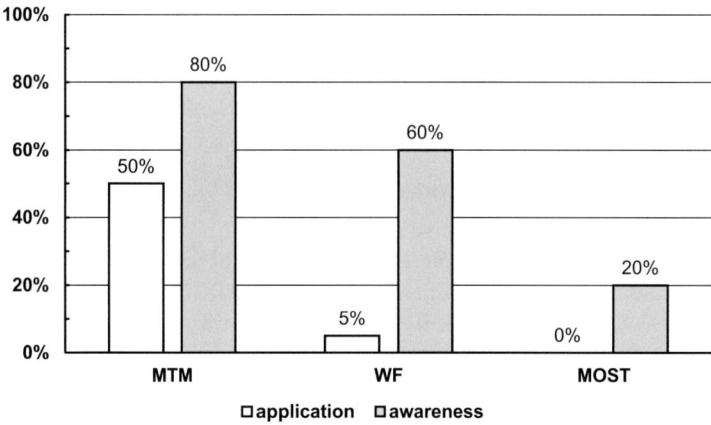

Figure 5.2: Share of application and awareness for different motion time systems (Sautter et al. 1998, 47)

These other systems, like SD (Standard Data), UAS (Universal Analysing System) and SVL (Standard logistic processes), aggregate basic movements of the MTM basic system to basic processes or operations, which results in a reduced analysing effort, and at the same time leads to more general values (Heinz and Olbrich 1989, 15). On the other hand, this can also be a disadvantage if a high accuracy is necessary, as also influencing parameters have been consolidated to get more general values (Crostack et al. 2007, 51). But in our case, we want to calculate capacity in a long term and according to references of Heinz and Olbrich (1989, 53), for this purpose the accuracy between real values and analysed target values is sufficient between 13 and 20 percent, as higher accuracy would also lead to higher efforts needed for analysing. This effort does not make sense in this stage, as for example the final layout of the system is not yet clear and/or the conditions given by customer orders are only forecasts. Both lead to inaccuracy anyhow and therefore, we can use these general values.

In order to calculate general times for the specifications of influencing parameters identified in the morphological boxes (cf. Section 5.2), we take aggregated movements, preferably of the SVL system, as boundary conditions of logistics have been considered. If there is no equivalent process or operation given in SVL, also UAS, SD and MTM basic system are used alternatively. MEK is not relevant, as it is specialised for individual production (Bokranz and Landau 2006, 513), which is not the case in packing areas.

5.3.2 Analysis of Variance

As mentioned before, we want to use analysis of variance (ANOVA) in order to determine the significance of the influencing parameters. With this analysis the total variability is partitioned into its component parts (Montgomery 2009, 66), and we can find out if the parameter under investigation affects the result with a certain probability (Hartung et al. 2009, 609 and Krottmaier 1994, 37). If this probability is high, the parameter should definitely be considered in the cycle time formulas. Non significant values can be deferred, as their influence on time necessary to perform is negligible (cf. REFA 1997, 351).

Alternatively to the analysis of variance, we considered the concept of complete enumeration. This approach, however, is infeasible due to the number of possible combinations (136,069 for each of the nine morphological boxes considering all specifications and 64 for each box for only the two extreme specifications). Each possibility in the tree needs to be modelled using MTM times and no design of experiments can be used to reduce the effort needed.

Another idea was to perform a sensitivity analysis. We decide not to use it. No mathematical descriptions exist to calculate results while varying the input, but we need to model the cases using MTM. This means that we also have effects among parameter combinations and we would not

5.3 Analysis of the Morphological Boxes

be able to assign the result to the effect of one parameter. Additionally, when performing the sensitivity analysis for different specifications of a parameter, we would need a method to decide on the combination of sensitivity effects. The analysis of different specifications would be necessary to avoid picking a non-significant specification whereas another specification is significant.

Further, we considered regression analysis which is more appropriate when using continuous process parameters only, not discrete ones or a mixture (Dietrich and Alfred 2010, 409).

Another option considered was factor analysis, which also uses a covariance matrix as a basis for the analysis as the analysis of variance. To reduce parameters using a factor analysis, a decision on a method is required and this choice influences the number of parameters which are considered relevant. Therefore, it is often recommended to use several methods and decide by a combination of these which parameters are significant. This procedure does not seem to be as objective as the analysis of variance. As a result, we want to use the analysis of variance and describe how we proceed in the following.

To study the effects of the parameters in the morphological boxes identified in Section 5.2, we need to decide on the design of experiments. If the significance of parameters should be identified, often only the two extreme specifications are regarded (Siebertz et al. 2010, 132). This leads to two levels, and therefore two cases to be modelled with MTM for each parameter. As every box contains in average six parameters, a full factorial design would lead to $2^6 = 64$ combinations (Montgomery 2009, 289) to be modelled per box, with nine boxes in total. For each box only six of the 63 degrees of freedom would correspond to the parameters. 15 correspond to interactions between two parameters, all the others are for interactions between more parameters (Montgomery 2009, 289). This kind of design is usually used if interactions are important and need to be quantified separately, which it is not true in our case, as it is sort of a screening experiment (Montgomery 2009, 290).

But also fractional factorial designs have been developed. In these designs the number of combinations is equal to a full factorial, but the amount of parameters increases (Kleppmann 2011, 123). The 2^{k-p} fractional factorial designs contain a $1/2^p$ fraction of the complete 2^k design, where p refers to the number of independent generators and k to the number of parameters (Montgomery 2009, 309). Fractional factorial designs are of different resolutions ($k - p$), and the highest resolution possible should be chosen for an experiment (Montgomery 2009, 309) in order to reduce the effects of interactions (for details cf. Taguchi 1987, 185). In our case, resolution III designs are used, as they are helpful for screening (Kleppmann 2011, 139, 239). This is due to the fact, that $k = N - 1$ parameters can be investigated in only N runs, where N has to be a multiple of four (Montgomery 2009, 320). We mainly use a 2_{III}^{7-4} design, which can be also used for less than seven parameters, simply by dropping any one column (Montgomery 2009, 321).

These are the reasons why we decided to use fractional factorial designs and in the following we summarise the main steps of the analysis of variance. For details, we refer to Kleppmann (2011), Siebertz, van Bebber and Hochkirchen (2010), Montgomery (2009) and Lindman (1992).

According to Siebertz et al. (2010, 108), the degrees of freedom within the analysis are distributed as follows:

- Parameters with a levels have $a - 1$ degrees of freedom (so in our case with two levels ($a = 2$) each parameter has one ($df_X = 1$)),

- The whole design of experiment with N runs has $N - 1$ degrees of freedom ($df_T = N - 1$), and

- The difference between the total degrees of freedom and the sum of degrees of freedom of the parameters are the degrees of freedom of the error ($df_E = N - 1 - \sum_{i=1}^{k} (a - 1)$). (cf. also Montgomery 2009, 228)

In order to measure the total variability in data, the corrected sum of squares SS_T can be used (Montgomery 2009, 66):

$$\begin{aligned} SS_T &= \sum_{i=1}^{a} \sum_{j=1}^{n} (y_{ij} - \bar{y}_{..})^2 \\ &= n \sum_{i=1}^{a} (\bar{y}_{i.} - \bar{y}_{..})^2 + \sum_{i=1}^{a} \sum_{j=1}^{n} (y_{ij} - \bar{y}_{i.})^2 \end{aligned} \quad (5.1)$$

5.3 Analysis of the Morphological Boxes

Divided by the number of degrees of freedom of the experiment $(N-1)$, it results in the sample variance. The second equation shows that the sum can be partitioned into the differences between treatment averages ($SS_{Treatments}$) and within these (SS_E) (Montgomery 2009, 66), where SS_E is caused by random errors.

In order to determine whether a parameter is significant and to which degree, hypothesis testing is used (for details on hypothesis testing we refer to Montgomery (2009, 34-41)).The null hypothesis is that there are no differences in treatment means ($H_0 : \tau_1 = ... = \tau_a = 0$) (Montgomery 2009, 69). This means that the parameter does not affect the result more than by a random deviation when varied (Siebertz et al. 2010, 111). So in our case, we want to reject the null hypothesis in order to show the significance of a parameter.

In order to determine this, we calculate the ratio

$$F_0 = \frac{SS_{Treatments}/(a-1)}{SS_E/\left(N-1-\sum_{i=1}^{k}(a-1)\right)} = \frac{MS_{Treatments}}{MS_E} \quad (5.2)$$

which is distributed as a F distribution with $(a-1)$ and $(N-1-\sum_{i=1}^{k}(a-1))$ degrees of freedom (cf. Montgomery 2009, 69). F_0 refers to the calculated value of the respective parameter of investigation.

We can use this distribution if all measurements are independent, normally distributed with a mean of $\mu + \tau_i$ and an identical variance σ^2 per level (Siebertz et al. 2010, 113). But even if this would not be the case, results of the analysis of variance can still be used descriptively (Toutenburg et al. 2009, 239), as the F test is robust against nonnormality and unequal variances (cf. Lindman 1992, 21-23, 32).

We can reject the null hypothesis if

$$F_0 > F_{\alpha, a-1, N-1-\sum_{i=1}^{k}(a-1)} \quad (5.3)$$

(cf. Montgomery 2009, 69). Here α refers to the so called level of significance, which can be chosen according to the required accuracy. We use the 1, 5 and 10 percent level of significance in this thesis. As already mentioned, a parameter effect is significant to the respective level if it is not compatible with the null hypothesis of a random deviation (Siebertz et al. 2010, 120).

To gain a better understanding of how big the parameter influence is as a share of the total corrected sum of squares,

$$p_{Treatment} = \frac{SS_{Treatment}}{SS_T} \cdot 100[\%] \qquad (5.4)$$

can be calculated. $p_{Treatment}$ shows the percentage that can be accounted for by the variation of the levels of the respective parameter (Siebertz et al. 2010, 108).

In order to show all the results in a standardised and summarised way, an ANOVA table can be used (cf. e.g. Table 5.12, Montgomery 2009, 70 and Krottmaier 1994, 39). This table is used in the following section, where we use the analysis combined with predetermined motion time systems in order determine the significance of the parameters.

5.3.3 Results from Analysis of Variance

After introducing the methods of predetermined motion time systems (Section 5.3.1) and the analysis of variance (Section 5.3.2), in this section we want to present the results of the ANOVA analysis for the morphological boxes introduced in Section 5.2. Our approach to analyse effects shall be illustrated in detail using the morphological box of preparing the job. For the other processes we will only present a summary and the results.

As described in Section 5.3.2, first of all the extreme specifications have to be chosen and every parameter is assigned to a letter. The resulting table, with abbreviations, parameters, and their two extreme levels of specification can be seen in Table 5.10.

In the original box, we had nine influencing parameters, some of them with sub specifications, and here we list only eight. We decided to analyse common parameters, which are part of several process steps like the weight of items, only once to reduce the effort for analysing. We show results of the analysis of the common parameters right after inquiring on preparing the job. To come back to prepare the job, this means we

5.3 Analysis of the Morphological Boxes

Abbr.	Influencing parameter	Specification 1	Specification 2
A	Items handling	one hand	moving required with device
B	Choose job	not required	specified job
C	Confirmation on start	not required	manual
D	Identification	not required	manual comparison
E	Transport of items to workplace	not required	manual with device, single items
F	Decision on packaging	provided proposal	packer's decision
G	Decision on protection material	not required	packer's decision
H	Decision on securing method	provided proposal	packer's decision

Table 5.10: Parameters with analysed specifications for 'prepare job'

dropped the influencing parameter of item weight and assumed the items to be transported separately.

As mentioned in Section 5.3.2, in a 2_{III}^{7-4} fractional factorial design a maximum of seven parameters can be used. So in this case of eight parameters we have to use a 2_{III}^{15-11} design, in order to be able to analyse all parameters. Accordingly, we have to drop the unnecessary columns (cf. Montgomery 2009, 321). In the first column of Table 5.11 we can see the number of the respective run and to the right the parameter abbreviations. These columns indicate the respective level within the run. The last column in Table 5.11 shows the time necessary for the parameter combination with the indicated levels. This time is determined by performing one run for each of the 16 combinations and modelling the time using the predetermined motion times of MTM. This is also the reason for time being measured in TMU (Time Measurement Unit), where one TMU equals 0.036 seconds (cf. MTM 2004). Further, the sums of times when the respective parameter is on level 1 and respectively 2, as

well as the average of total times over the 16 runs, and the corrected sum
of squares are given.

Run	A	B	C	D	E	F	G	H	Time [TMU]
1	1	1	1	1	1	1	1	1	50
2	1	1	1	1	1	2	2	2	385
3	1	1	1	2	2	1	1	1	715
4	1	1	1	2	2	2	2	2	1050
5	1	2	2	1	2	1	2	2	1250
6	1	2	2	1	2	2	1	1	1070
7	1	2	2	2	1	1	2	2	925
8	1	2	2	2	1	2	1	1	745
9	2	1	2	1	1	1	1	2	455
10	2	1	2	1	1	2	2	1	635
11	2	1	2	2	2	1	1	2	1395
12	2	1	2	2	2	2	2	1	1575
13	2	2	1	1	2	1	2	1	1320
14	2	2	1	1	2	2	1	2	1295
15	2	2	1	2	1	1	2	1	720
16	2	2	1	2	1	2	1	2	695
SumX = 1	6190	6260	6230	6460	4610	6830	6420	6830	
SumX = 2	8090	8020	8050	7820	9670	7450	7860	7450	
$\bar{y}_{..}$									893
SS_T									2595350

Table 5.11: 2_{III}^{15-11} fractional factorial design for 'prepare job'

These are intermediate results, used to calculate the inputs necessary for the
ANOVA Table 5.12 according to the formulas introduced in Section 5.3.2.

The value of the F distribution for $\alpha = 0.1$, $df_X = 1$ and $df_E = 7$ is 3.59.
If F_0 is larger than 3.59, the parameter is significant with a probability
of 90 percent. According to Table 5.12, this is the case for parameter B
(Choosing job) and C (Confirmation on start) as well as A (Unit handling)

5.3 Analysis of the Morphological Boxes

	df	SS$_X$	MS$_X$	F_0	p	sign. level
A	1	225625	225625	5.59	8.69%	5%
B	1	193600	193600	4.79	7.46%	10%
C	1	207025	207025	5.13	7.98%	10%
D	1	115600	115600	2.86	4.45%	
E	1	1600225	1600225	39.63	61.66%	1%
F	1	24025	24025	0.59	0.93%	
G	1	129600	129600	3.21	4.99%	
H	1	24025	24025	0.59	0.93%	
Error	7	282650	40379			

Table 5.12: ANOVA table for 'prepare job'

and E (Transport of items to workplace). But we also have one parameter A (Unit handling), which is significant with a probability of 95 percent ($F_0 \geq 5.59$) and a parameter E (Transport), which is significant with a probability of 99 percent ($F_0 \geq 8.07$).

In the following, we summarise the results:

- As mentioned before, p indicates the share of the parameter on the total effect (cf. formula 5.4). As we already described, transport influences preparing the job the most. This is already indicated by the significance level, but it can also be realised by the p value of 61.66 percent.

- The second most important parameter is the item size, followed by the activities of choosing the job and confirming the start. Their influence does not differ a lot, as one can conclude from the p values, but because the F_0 value is slightly higher, they do not share the same significance level.

- All other parameters are less important, as the significance analysis did not show a significance level higher than 90 percent, and their p-value is between 0.93 and 4.45 percent. This seems to be very reasonable, as the activities performed by the packer are very similar:

he mainly he has to decide about something. On the other hand for the more important parameters he needs to do something, which is more time consuming.

As mentioned before, we did this kind of analysis analogue for all morphological boxes, and separately for common influencing parameters. For all these, we just show the results using ANOVA tables and summarise the key findings in the following. In Section 5.4, we finally refine the morphological boxes.

For preparing the job, 16 runs have been necessary to determine the influence of parameters, as parameters exceed the number of seven. Therefore, we did one separate 2_{III}^{7-4} experiment for all sub-processes to analyse the influence of common parameters (cf. Table 5.13), like weight, number of units handled together (batching) and distance of the transport. For the weight we used lighter than one and heavier than 22 kg as specifications. For the number of units handled together, we choose a single unit transport, and a combined transport of four units. The distance of transport was varied between 3 m (which we use as a single distance in all later cases) and 12 m. Another reason for doing this analysis separately was to avoid too many interferences, which would distort the results. Regarding the results in the ANOVA Table 5.13 we can see that

- Weight has a relatively small influence and was not even significant to the 90 percent level in this analysis.

- The combination of units in handling influences the results with a probability of 90 percent and influence in this analysis was 33.77 percent.

- The biggest impact is the transport distance with 46.76 percent. We assumed in Section 4.1 that for efficiency the packer should not leave his workplace, and therefore we concentrate on 'short transports' from a supply area to the workplace. As this parameter influences results so much and we want to avoid bias at all, we fix the distance for the following experiments at 3m.

For preparing the packaging, we again used a 2_{III}^{15-11} design, as we have more than seven parameters. Investigating Table 5.14 we can conclude the following:

5.3 Analysis of the Morphological Boxes

	df	SS_X	MS_X	F_0	p	sign. level
Weight	1	12800	12800	0.94	3.69%	
Batching	1	117007	117007	8.56	33.77%	5%
Transport distance	1	162023	162023	11.85	46.76%	5%
Error	4	54698	13674			

Table 5.13: ANOVA table for 'common parameters'

	df	SS_X	MS_X	F_0	p	sign. level
Packaging handling	1	392458	392458	18.30	15.44%	1%
Packaging material provision	1	237154	237154	11.06	9.33%	5%
Positioning of packaging	1	26724	26724	1.25	1.05%	
Set up packaging	1	105057	105057	4.90	4.13%	10%
Fix joints	1	92827	92827	4.33	3.65%	10%
Open packaging	1	33133	33133	1.55	1.30%	
Assemble loading unit	1	1482245	1482245	69.13	58.33%	1%
Error	8	171541	21443			

Table 5.14: ANOVA table for 'prepare packaging'

- The most important process is the assembling of the unit (99 percent probability of significance, 58.33 percent impact). This is very time consuming, but not often necessary as mainly standardised packaging is used (only 4 percent of the areas use not standardised packaging, cf. Weiblen and Berbig 2011). Therefore, we do not consider this parameter while refining the morphological boxes to a condensed one.

- The second most important parameter, with also 99 percent probability of significance, is the size of the packaging with 15.44 percent impact. For preparing the job, we already identified the significant parameter of handling items, now we realise that also handling of the packaging is important.

- The location of the material is important on the five percent significance level. The parameter depends on the distance between workplace and location, like we have realised for transport.
- Two other parameters are significant with 90 percent probability: Set up the packaging and fixing the joints. Both are mainly necessary for corrugated containers only. We modelled fixing the joints using tape, as this is the most common way in industry (50 percent of the cases, cf. Weiblen and Berbig 2011).

	df	SS_X	MS_X	F_0	p	sign. level
Packaging handling	1	11766	11766	26.15	0.79%	
Item handling	1	1268825	1268825	2819.61	85.33%	5%
Type of items	1	51200	51200	113.78	3.44%	10%
Item stability	1	25674	25674	57.05	1.73%	10%
Order of items	1	84050	84050	186.78	5.65%	5%
Positioning items	1	45000	45000	100.00	3.03%	10%
Error	1	450	450			

Table 5.15: ANOVA table for 'pack'

Packing depends on the number of articles that need to be packed, which we wanted to take into account by using a factor later in the formula, as it correctly reflects this input without creating additional complexity. Therefore, we did not investigate the number of articles per shipping unit with the analysis of variance. Based on Table 5.15 we can summarise:

- The size of items is important, whereas the size of the packaging is not even significant and influences only 0.79 percent. This can be explained by the fact that each item needs to be handled and therefore the packer might even need to move, whereas for the packaging he only needs to handle it once to put it at the right location.

5.3 Analysis of the Morphological Boxes

- Even though the order of items is on the same significance level as the item size (95 percent probability of significance), we realise that the p value with 5.65 percent is closer to the ones of the other parameters (all smaller than 3.44 percent) than to the dimensions of the items (85.33 percent).

- The other parameters (stability, type and positioning of items) are all significant with 90 percent probability. But, as mentioned, their share is very small compared to the share of the item handling.

	df	SS_X	MS_X	F_0	p	sign. level
Item handling	1	161881	161881	159.88	13.58%	10%
Amount check	1	12800	12800	12.64	1.07%	
Identity check	1	72200	72200	71.31	6.06%	10%
Volume check	1	383688	383688	378.95	31.19%	5%
Quality inspection	1	486098	486098	480.10	40.79%	5%
Confirmation	1	74113	74113	73.20	6.22%	10%
Error	1	1013	1013			

Table 5.16: ANOVA table for 'check'

For checking, the following findings based on Table 5.16 can be made:

- Quality inspection is very time consuming, even though we modelled a basic case of assessing the condition of the product packing, which is the usual case selection as per our observations within the research project. The other checks, apart from the amount check, are also time consuming, and either significant with 95 or 90 percent probability.

- For checking, the size of the items matters, even though only to the 10 percent significance level.

- Else, the confirmation has a significant influence. Partly, the reason therefore is that we modelled it manually and per unit, which means the packer has to check off every single unit of the order by using a pen. We used this scenario, because we simulated the two extreme specifications and signing is very time consuming. As a result, the share of the effect is 6.22 percent.

	df	SS_X	MS_X	F_0	p	sign. level
Unit handling	1	12137	12137	5.11	8.78%	
Access to unit	1	10893	10893	4.59	7.88%	
Protection material provision	1	60205	60205	23.37	43.54%	1%
Type of protection material	1	47926	47926	20.19	34.66%	1%
Error	3	7120	2373			

Table 5.17: ANOVA table for 'protect'

We analysed four parameters for protecting the unit. This is because we use MTM and the degree of automation for handling the protection material has to be manual. Only two out of the four parameters are significant with more than 90 percent probability, but therefore with 99 percent (cf. Table 5.17):

- The biggest impact with a share of 43.54 percent is the provision of material.

- Further, the material used to protect the items is important. Of course, there might be restrictions, either necessary to obey due to the items characteristics, or because for example the customer only accepts a special type. But due to the importance, it should be well chosen.

- The other parameters, unit size and access to packaging, did slightly not pass the significance level of 10 percent.

Based on Table 5.18, we can summarise the insertion of add-ins as follows:

- Similar to the results we discussed for packing, and for the same reasons, also inserting add-ins depends mainly on the size of the item and how well it can be handled (95 percent probability of significance, share of 40.75).

5.3 Analysis of the Morphological Boxes

	df	SS_X	MS_X	F_0	p	sign. level
Add-in handling	1	82013	82013	262.44	40.75%	5%
Add-in provision	1	37813	37813	121.00	18.79%	10%
Add-in position	1	23328	23328	74.65	11.59%	10%
Initialisation print	1	25088	25088	80.28	12.47%	10%
Fold	1	24775	24775	79.28	12.31%	10%
Inserting bag	1	7938	7938	25.40	3.94%	
Error	3	312	312			

Table 5.18: ANOVA table for 'insert add-in'

- The other parameters, apart from inserting the add-in into a bag, are only significant to the 10 percent level, with the provision in reach or out of reach as the most important parameter among them with a share of 18.79 percent. The share of the other three parameters is only around 12 percent.

	df	SS_X	MS_X	F_0	p	sign. level
Unit handling	1	29078517	29078517	80614	43.86%	1%
Securing material provision	1	46872	46872	130	0.07%	1%
Working area	1	298662	298662	828	0.45%	1%
Close package	1	28612	28612	79	0.04%	1%
Fix joints	1	83723	83723	232	0.13%	1%
Strap unit	1	7731180	7731180	21433	11.66%	1%
Stretch wrap unit	1	7563050	7563050	20967	11.41%	1%
Shrink wrap unit	1	18380941	18380941	50957	27.73%	1%
Error	7	2525	361			

Table 5.19: ANOVA table for 'secure'

Securing also needs a 2_{III}^{15-11} design due to the amount of parameters. As times for securing by strapping, stretching or shrinking are relatively high, but the error is low, all parameters are significant to the one percent level (cf. Table 5.19). Therefore, we focus on the p-values, when we conclude the following:

- The most important parameter is the unit size with a share of 43.86 percent. This is obvious as for all securing methods we need to handle the unit.

- The next group includes the three securing methods, and the way they are performed. Thereof, shrink wrapping is the most time consuming if performed manually.

- This time transport, like for the provision of securing out of reach or the travel time to the central area, carries less weight, as securing itself is so time consuming.

- The other parameters have a very low share of 0.04 to 0.13 percent.

	df	SS_X	MS_X	F_0	p	sign. level
Marking material provision	1	55811	55811	1.92	11.04%	
Initialisation print	1	55811	55811	1.92	11.04%	
Mark	1	220514	220514	7.57	43.62%	10%
Method	1	86113	86113	2.96	17.03%	
Error	3	87337	29113			

Table 5.20: ANOVA table for 'mark'

For marking, we analysed four parameters, provision of material, initialisation of print and marking, where we distinguished, apart from degree of automation, between attaching a self adhesive label and directly writing the information on the shipping unit. Results are shown in ANOVA Table 5.20.

- The analysis results in one significant parameter with 90 percent probability, which is the degree of automation for marking.

- The other parameters have a share of the total corrected sum of squares between 11 and 17 percent, but do not reach a significant level.

	df	SS_X	MS_X	F_0	p	sign. level
Unit handling	1	76714	76714	17.73	29.93%	5%
Confirmation on end	1	19503	19503	4.51	7.61%	
Clear workspace	1	24753	24753	5.72	9.66%	10%
Transport of units to provision area	1	122364	122364	28.29	47.74%	5%
Error	3	12977	4326			

Table 5.21: ANOVA table for 'provide'

The last analysis is on providing the shipping unit. The details are shown in Table 5.21, and we summarise the following:

- As for preparing the job, the most significant parameters are the size of the unit and the transport. Both are significant to the 5 percent level and here as well transport has a bigger share.

- The degree of automation for clearing the workplace is also significant, but only to the 10 percent level. With 9.66 percent the share is close to the one of confirmation, which is not significant for this process step.

In the following chapter, we summarise and discuss the previously given results and reduce the morphological boxes to a combined one. Additionally, we highlight implications for cycle time derivation.

5.4 Refining the Solution and Implications for Cycle Time

In the previous section, we have described the results of analysing the morphological boxes for each process step. We also realised that the results depend a lot on activities performed within the operation of a process step and their time consumption. For some steps, we could not easily identify the most significant parameters, as times and therefore also significance levels were equally distributed along the parameters. Other process steps showed relatively clear results. Anyhow, we can use all results as indicators for the significance of the parameters.

As introduced at the beginning of this chapter, we now want to try to reduce the number of parameters to the significant ones and as a result are going to create a condensed morphological box. For these parameters, we can derive implications for the cycle time, which we consider in Chapter 6.

As Sarker and Babu (1995, 174-175) mention, it is impossible to incorporate all the parameters in a single model of cycle times. We have seen for picking (cf. Section 2.3.3) that there is a general formula, which has be refined for various combinations of the characteristics by different researchers. For packing as well, we have to consider which characteristics can be summarised in a general formula, and which are possibilities we do have to categorise characteristics in order to refine this general formula.

In the following, we want to summarise the results of the analysis and discuss which implications can be drawn for the cycle time.

The size of any handling unit, whether it was packaging material, a package, an item, an add-in or the ready to be shipped unit, has proofed to be a significant influencing parameter. To reduce the morphological boxes, we combine all parameters to the parameter 'unit handling', as specifications for the respective unit did not differ anyhow. We also learned that, especially for packing and securing, the item size was a significant parameter. This has even more importance, because we mentioned for packing that we need a factor to model different 'lot sizes' (cf. Section 5.3.3) and packing times have to be multiplied by a factor. As it is not possible to determine a general equation including the influence of the size of a unit in a general formula, but size has a large influence on respective values, we could use this parameter to differentiate specifications of the general formula. Item and shipping unit size have been the most significant parameters, and usually add-ins or packaging for example are chosen according to these sizes. Anyhow, the two parameters should be considered when modelling tasks. Thereby, tasks should require a similar amount of effort to be

5.4 Refining the Solution and Implications for Cycle Time

accomplished and be comparable, because they have the same starting and end status. This structure is developed in Chapter 7.

Another important parameter throughout the analysis was the transport of items and shipping units. This is the most significant parameter for 'preparing the job' and 'provide', respectively. Within the analysis of common parameters we found that it is also significant how many items are transported together, and that transport highly depends on the distance. All this leads to the conclusion that transport should be modelled using cycle times and factors should give the possibility to take distance and combined transport of several items into account. Additionally, there was one further transport: if there is a central area for securing and units have to be transported there. This was significant to the 99 percent level, as all parameters in securing, because the error was so small. It had the biggest share after the securing methods and the unit size. Combined with the findings of analysing common parameters, we recommend including it in the cycle time calculation. This is especially important, because it is usually part of each packing cycle and cannot be combined for several shipping units, which means for example that after building the pallet the packer leaves his workplace for each of them to secure it.

As already mentioned, analysing the common parameters showed that combining units or items to accomplish an activity is significant. There, the purpose was combining units for transport, but also for packing items and inserting add-ins we distinguished if they are handled together or one by one (cf. Table 5.3 and 5.6). Therefore, we include the parameter batching which refers to the handling of units together or to the handling of each single unit individually.

Also the provision of different materials was generally an important parameter, especially for protection material. One could argue, that if these are not provided within reach, a transport is necessary. On the other hand if they are provided in reach, no transport is required which could be modelled in a calculation by setting the distance to zero. Therefore, both cases could be reflected with a transport calculation. We already realised how transport varies with the number of items transported together as well as on the distance. For replenishment of material we have identified further influencing parameters, which could be significant as well. Examples are stops, picking of material, frequency of transport for provision, etc. We also emphasised that, for value-adding purposes, the packer should not leave his workplace and therefore transport activities to be accomplished by him should be avoided. All this leads to the conclusion that the supply with material out of reach, like for protection material, is very particular and depends a lot on the local set-up (cf. Dzeik and Picker 2003, 68). Further, it is not a standard activity within packing, which needs to be performed within one packing cycle, as it could be performed for several orders together. Therefore, we suggest not trying to assume these activities within a general formula, but we suppose that material is within reach or located at the packing workplace. Eventually, some necessary steps or turns should be included within the respective time of performing the activity. Consequently, we do not include it in the morphological box, as significance depends on importance within the different sub-processes.

According to Meier (2005, 111), we should also try to combine specifications to new categories. In the analysis, we found out that when checking items, the parameters describing the type of the check, especially the volume and quality check, were equally significant and their share in influence was similar. So the idea is to summarise all types of checking to a new parameter, where the specifications are amount, identity, volume and quality check, which is completed by the possibility of 'not required'. For the cycle time, this means we need to model one part with a fixed factor, which can be adapted according to the respective specification. Again, we need to multiply it with the number of items inserted or a share of it, depending on the sample size. Accordingly, we also proceeded for the securing method, which we summarise to one parameter. We add not required, closing and fixing joints to the specifications of strap, stretch wrap and shrink wrap unit, because even though they showed no big significance they are typical for small loads, and need to be included.

In order to reduce the morphological boxes, we proceed like mentioned at the beginning of Chapter 5.3. Thereby, we focus on actions that are very time consuming and therefore significant, and defer parameters of low importance. Due to the combination of specifications to new categories, the result is less specific. One example for this is the degree of automation, which influences performance and parameters a lot, especially the combined ones. Therefore, we also combine all specifications of automation for different parameters, and get one influencing parameter 'degree of automation'. Whenever the packing actions do not share the same degree of automation,

5.4 Refining the Solution and Implications for Cycle Time

the overall degree is hard to distinguish. Nevertheless, differences in the degree of automation do not necessarily mean a difference in the general cycle time formulas, but can be used as differentiation criterion to refine the formulas. This is why we do not need to handle or structure the degree of automation for different actions separately. The difference only has an impact later on, when a specific value needs to be determined. In this case, we can use MTM for manual processes and times which are provided by the manufacturer for machines or calculate the respective value with a specific formula, for example.

So far, we achieved a condensed morphological box of five parameters, but for protecting we did not consider the most significant parameters. For protecting, the most significant parameter was the provision of material. But as discussed above, all provision tasks should be avoided, thus not necessary, as the packer should stay at his workplace. Therefore, we do not want to consider it in the cycle time. The second most important parameter, with a share of 34.66 percent, is the protection material type. This must be included in the condensed morphological box. For the time calculation, different protection material types influence the time necessary, but at the same time need to be calculated differently as well. Therefore, it would be hard to find a general formula to calculate times for protecting and we suggest a fixed parameter, which has to be calculated according to the system in place.

The only other very significant parameter, which we did not consider so far, is the assembling of the packaging. But again, this is a very specific case of packing and there is no benefit including it in the morphological box. Anyhow, the general formulas for cycle time calculations should also be valid for this specific case and we use this case to increase the credibility of applying the the formulas for different cases later on (cf. Section 7.4).

All other parameters either had a lower significance level or a smaller share, so that we defer them for the condensed morphological box including all process steps. The resulting morphological box with the six most influencing parameters is shown in Table 5.22.

Apart from being useful for us to determine general cycle time formulas and structure the packing process, this box also shows which parameters need to be considered in particular, when planning or optimising a packing system. A reduction in time necessary to perform one of the operations

Unit handling	one hand	both hands	moving required			
			no device	device		
Transport	not required/ auto- mated	semi- automated	manual			
			no device	device		
Batching	several units together	single units				
Type of check	not required	amount	identity	volume	quality	
Securing method	not required	close	fix joints	strap	stretch wrap	shrink wrap
Degree of automation	automated	semi- automated	manual			
Type of protection material	not required	loose/ liquid material	piece material	yard material		

Table 5.22: Resulting condensed morphological box for packing

represented by these parameters will have a much higher impact on the whole packing process, when being compared to parameters that are not listed. This also implies that it is most beneficial to start automating the most significant operations first.

6 Determining Cycle Times for Packing

In this chapter, we use the knowledge gained in the previous ones in order to determine cycle times for packing in distribution centres. In the first section, we determine a basic structure of the cycle time formula, which we then further detail in its single components.

In order to formulate general cycle time formulas, we need to make some assumptions about the system. We assume that:

- We consider time averages, even though we know that parameters vary, so calculations are an approximation. If variation is too high, parameters should be grouped for investigation and calculation performed for each of the groups separately (cf. Gudehus 1973, 44).

- We do not consider any strategies and do not specify workstation layouts, as formulas we determine should be generally valid.

- Formulas do not include a factor for availability (unproductive times, technical downtimes, personal need allowance, non-packing related secondary work) and usability (waiting due to congestions, for information, or supply) (cf. Gudehus 2011, 744-745 and Radtke 2000, 72).

- If waiting or standby times occur for the packer while waiting for an automated process to finish, this time must be included in the respective sub-process time share.

- If operations or activities are performed in parallel, the longer one has to be considered while the shorter one has to be set to zero (cf. Gudehus 2011, 739). This is necessary due to the use of summation operators.

- The packing area realises the packing process as described in Chapter 2.2 and we do not consider pick and pack processes, for example.
- If process steps or activities are not performed at all, the respective time components must be set to zero.
- Supplying activities for consumables, like replenishing packaging, securing, protecting materials and add-ins etc., are not part of the packing process and are not considered. They are described by the availability of a system, since they are non-packing related secondary activities (cf. Gudehus 2011, 744).
- Times for operations or activities can be analysed by observing a system, determined by using predetermined motion time systems or formulas, or can be given as part of the machine specifications by the manufacturer, depending on the degree of automation.
- For values indicated in the following sections, the conditions given by the respective MTM system need to be obeyed.
- Distances must include both, outward and return travel.

These assumptions apply for the determination of cycle times in the following sections. For deriving times for this process, we build upon established cycle time formulas in picking (cf. Section 2.3.3) and make packing-specific modifications based on the previous chapters with focus on the analysis of Chapter 5 to achieve general formulas for packing.

6.1 Cycle Time General Formula

As we have seen in previous chapters, times necessary to perform a process depend on many factors and parameters. In Section 2.3.2 we learned that usually cycle times are divided in variable and constant time components. This also applies to picking times, as we have seen in Section 2.3.3 and also the formula of Radtke (2000) can be divided into constant and variable parts. Therefore, we follow this common approach and divide the general formula for packing into these two components:

$$t_{pack} = t_{var} + t_{const} \tag{6.1}$$

6.1 Cycle Time General Formula

The variable part of the packing time t_{var} includes time necessary to transport items, reach a shared facility, and transport the finished packing unit. It makes sense to separate all transport processes from other activities, as they highly influence time, and depend very much on the respective system in place (cf. Section 5.3), as well as on the applied strategy (cf. Borcherdt 1994, 32). As in picking formulas transport processes are referred to as 'travel time', we want to use the same expression for packing. Therefore, t_{var} equals t_{travel}.

For picking, the constant part or dwell time (t_{const}) is divided into 'set-up time', 'base time' and 'picking time' (cf. Section 2.3.3), which is again similar to Radtke (2000). He divides the base time further into a part for preparing and a part for finishing the order. If we use the picking scheme and apply it to the identified sub-processes for packing (cf. Figure 4.2), it results in the following structure:

- Set-up time (t_{set-up}): Prepare job and mark
- Base time (t_{base}): Prepare packaging, protect, insert add-in, secure and provide
- Item time (t_{item}): Pack and check

On the one hand, the structure is based on the description which operations belong to which category for picking, as shown in Section 2.3.3. On the other hand, we analyse the multiplier of the time: item time depends on the amount of articles per order, whereas the other times occur once per order. Further, the two times included in the set-up time are mainly focused on information processing and do not depend as much on movements and measurements (cf. Section 5.3).

According to Gudehus (1973, 53), the set-up time should mainly focus on information based activities. As mentioned before, activities for preparing the job are information based. In Table 5.1 we listed choosing the job, confirming, identifying and deciding on packaging, protection material and securing method as information based activities and found out in Section 5.3 that they are almost equally significant. The other two significant parameters were transport and item handling. As all other parameters are information based and not based on physical material handling, the significance of item handling is mainly related to the transport of the items.

We included transport in the travel time, and therefore we assign 'prepare job' to the set-up time.

If units have to be marked, they are usually labelled (82.5 percent over all processes, Verpackungsprojekt 2011). The label is typically generated by printing it, but even for writing the address on the label or directly onto the unit information processing is an important task. Sticking the label on the unit needs comparably less time, and is part of the coding necessary for the information flow. Therefore, we also assign marking to the set-up time.

As mentioned before, all process steps summarised in the base time are only performed once per order. In picking, base time steps are often performed at a central workspace, before or after picking, and waiting times are not included (Gudehus 2011, 741). For packing, they are usually performed at the same workplace together with the other process steps. We have seen within the analysis of variance (cf. Section 5.3) that apart from transport, which is modelled separately, the dimensions of the respective unit are usually a significant influencing parameter. We discussed that this could be a parameter to classify packing in order to further detail this process. Additionally, the used method influences time, as particularly mentioned for protection and securing. Of course, it also depends on the system in place which steps need to be performed and how often. It might be possible that a unit needs to be taped first and strapped afterwards or that several add-ins have to be inserted. We need to consider this when deriving the more detailed time calculation for the base time. We can summarise that times included in the base time are very system dependent, which is also the case for picking (cf. Gudehus 1973, 55). Therefore, they should be distinguished for each system individually using predetermined motion time systems or measured on site (Gudehus 2011, 739).

Packing and checking are summarised by the item time, as they both depend on the number of items per shipping unit. Often, these steps are performed together. For example, when the item is grasped and lifted for packing, the packer checks the identification number before he places the item into or onto the packing unit. In contrast to picking, we include the time necessary to check the unit in the item time, because the time for checking needs to be multiplied by the number of articles per shipping unit as well. For packing and checking, the dimensions are important and transport is not relevant, as we have figured out in Section 5.3. Other influencing parameters, like the order of items or method of checking or confirmation depend on the system and can be considered when modelling the time share individually with motion time systems (cf. Gudehus 1973, 48).

For picking, time is measured per picking unit, which makes sense as orders might be handled together while picking and the picking unit is a fixed performance unit. For packing however, usually the output is given as performance indicator, for instance 10 parcels per hour, no matter how many articles are inside. Therefore, we suggest to measure packing of one shipping unit. In case that the time is needed to be indicated per packing position, one can still divide the packing time by the average number of positions.

Summarizing the above line of reasoning results in the following formula:

$$t_{packing} = t_{travel} + t_{set\text{-}up} + t_{base} + n \cdot t_{item} \qquad (6.2)$$

Where n refers to the number of articles per outgoing packing unit. In the following sections, we want to detail the single components and show how they can be calculated. Thereby, we consider the results mainly of Chapter 5. At the same time, we have to think of that we separated travel time in the formula above as an own component, and wanted to use the unit size as differentiating criterion later on. These two parameters have been the most significant ones throughout the analysis. Therefore, we include all activities, but only detail them according to significance.

6.2 Travel Time

As we have seen in the morphological boxes of Chapter 5, travelling of the packer is necessary for several operations and we identified this to be a significant parameter in Section 5.4. We also discussed that travelling of the packer should be generally avoided in order to increase productivity. Due to the significance, we suggest to include elements in the travel time to cater for provision and supply of the items and respectively shipping units, as well as transport to a central area. However, we do not include secondary supplying activities, like provision of packaging material, as we found out by a best bench approach that it is not recommendable to do so (Weiblen and Berbig 2012). Another point for their exclusion is that supplying processes vary a lot in terms of distance, number of stops, provision of material, transported amount, strategies etc., which would bias the travel time calculation (cf. Section 5.4).

It might be necessary that the packer fetches the items in a supply area (t_{t_supply}) and provides the finished shipping unit as well ($t_{t\_provide}$). If he can fetch all items for one shipping unit at the same time, we do not need to introduce a factor f_o (supply consolidation factor), which can be a multiplier or divisor. If he fetches every article separately, for instance, we need to multiply the travel time t_{t_supply} with the factor $f_o = n$. If he combines items for several shipping units on a trolley, we need use the factor f_o as a divisor, which includes the reciprocal of the average number of shipping units per transport.

We have similar cases for $t_{t\_provide}$, the provision of shipping units. Here, we only have two cases of transporting: every shipping unit separately, or combining some shipping units for transport. As the factor is different from f_o, as transported units usually differ, we use f_p (provision consolidation factor).

Often, some of the devices, especially for securing, are located in a central area and shared by several packers. Therefore, we introduce an additional term $t_{t\_central}$ to be able to model this case. Again, several shipping units might be combined for transport, and we represent these cases with the factor f_c (consolidation factor for transport to central area).

To calculate the individual travel times (t_{t_x}, where x refers to the respective operation), we can use the approximate formula following Gudehus (1973, 57):

$$t_{t\_x} = \frac{v}{b} + \frac{d}{v} + t_{pick} + t_{place} \tag{6.3}$$

Where v refers to the maximum velocity, b to the de-/acceleration constant and d to the travel distance. Gudehus (1973, 58) also indicates typical values for walking with and without load, using a trolley or powered pallet jack as well as automated material handling equipment, cf. Table 6.1. According to the degree of automation of the system, the right value has to be chosen.

6.2 Travel Time

We added time components to the travel time formula of Gudehus in Equitation 6.3, which covers the pick-up t_{pick} and placing of the unit or device t_{place}, as this is necessary each time something has to be transported. To pick up and place a single small load, MTM-UAS indicates 2.0 s (1-8 kg) or 4.1 s (8-22 kg) depending on the weight of the unit. To pick up a pallet with a pallet jack, values between 12.6 s and 22.1 s are given by MTM-SVL. Values to place units are assumed between 4.5 s and 11.2 s. For trolleys, pick up and placing is indicated with 1.3 s to 3.8 s in MTM-SVL. The corresponding values have to be chosen according to the local set-up and considering the influencing parameters given by the respective MTM method. For other systems, times need to be measured or looked up in the manufacturer manual.

Means of transport	De-/Acceleration [m/s^2]	Maximum velocity [m/s]
By foot (no load)	$b = 2.1 \pm 0.7$	$v = 1.4 \pm 0.2$
By foot (load up to 15kg)	$b = 1.3 \pm 0.4$	$v = 1.3 \pm 0.15$
By foot (with trolley up to 40kg)	$b = 1.3 \pm 0.4$	$v = 1.0 \pm 0.1$
By foot (with powered trolley, up to 1500kg)	$b = 0.8 \pm 0.2$	$v = 1.3 \pm 0.2$
Material handling equipment (up to 1000kg)	$b = 1.5 \pm 0.4$	$v = 2.6 \pm 0.2$
Lift truck (1000 to 2000kg)	$b = 1.1 \pm 0.3$	$v = 2.2 \pm 0.2$

Table 6.1: Typical de-/acceleration and velocity values following Gudehus (1973, 58)

If the throughput should be considered in completely automated systems, the conveying time can be calculated accordingly. If manpower in these systems should be considered, the travel time could be set to zero as it should not be necessary that the packer waits for automated transport. As mentioned, this formula (6.3) is approximating the travel time, as it assumes a constant value regardless if the transport is straight-lined or with curves, the latter being naturally slower. Additionally, with this formula we do not consider strategies or events like stopping at stations. If required, these cases have to be considered separately.

Alternatively, values can be calculated using MTM completely. With MTM, we do not need to consider de-/acceleration, as effects are included in the given constant value. Still, we have to differ between walking without device, which is given in SVL with 0.9 seconds per meter (cf. MTM-SVL), and with device. Here as well, we do have values for transportation per meter, but we have to consider curves separately. Therefore, we do not indicate values here, but refer to MTM-SVL.

To summarise, we can calculate the total travel time as the sum of the individual travel times for the operations, multiplied with the respective factor:

$$t_{travel} = f_o \cdot t_{t\_supply} + f_p \cdot t_{t\_provide} + f_c \cdot t_{t\_central} \qquad (6.4)$$

As a consequence, if the packer does not need to carry out one of the operations, the part for the respective operation has to be set to zero.

6.3 Set-up Time

We reasoned in Section 6.1, that the set-up time should include times for preparing the job and marking the shipping unit. We also found out, that times mainly concern information processing for these two process steps, as travel time is a separate time component of the basic formula.

In Section 5, we identified the activities necessary to perform these process steps and want to include them according to the significance. So to calculate set-up time, we have to add up times for choosing the job, confirming the start, identification, decision on packaging, decision on protection material, decision on securing material, initialisation of print and marking. For marking, we might need to add up several marking times, as the unit might require several labels, such as an address as well as a hazardous goods label.

To summarise, these considerations are represented in the following formula:

$$t_{set\text{-}up} = t_{choose} + t_{confirm} + t_{identify} + t_{d\_packaging} \\ + t_{d\_protect} + t_{d\_secure} + t_{print} + \sum t_{mark} \quad (6.5)$$

6.4 Base Time

Base times depend a lot on the respective system in place. But anyhow, we concluded in Section 6.1 that the activities summarised under prepare packaging, protecting, inserting add-in, securing as well as providing are included. Therefore, the base time needs to be calculated as follows:

$$t_{base} = t_{prepare} + t_{protect} + \sum t_{add\text{-}in} + \sum t_{secure} + t_{provide} \quad (6.6)$$

Here, we need to sum up times necessary to insert add-ins ($t_{add\text{-}in}$). We might have several add-ins and these add-ins might be different, a document and a gift for example, and therefore different times for insertion are necessary.

For securing, we need to have a sum over securing times as well, as we found out in Section 5.3 that the time for securing depends on closing the packaging, fixing the joints and/or one of the methods of strapping, stretching or shrink wrapping. In addition, several of these methods might be necessary for one shipping unit. Further, the methods differ in the required time, which depends on the technical implementation.

Again, we can use the results of Chapter 5 to identify possible activities that are necessary to perform the process steps added up in Formula 6.6. For preparing the packaging, we consider the time for setting up the packaging, fixing the joints and assembling of a loading unit as well as positioning and opening it.

$$t_{prepare} = t_{p\_set\text{-}up} + t_{p\_fixjoint} + t_{p\_assemble} + t_{p\_position} + t_{p\_open} \quad (6.7)$$

Volume, position, initialisation of the print and folding had significant influence on inserting an add-in. Time for inserting has to be determined depending on the size and position of an add-in, and eventually includes the insertion into a messenger bag. Further, times for printing as well as folding need to be added:

$$t_{add\text{-}in} = t_{a\_insert} + t_{a\_print} + t_{a\_fold} \qquad (6.8)$$

For protecting the unit, we analysed that it mainly depends on the method used, so we do not subdivide $t_{protect}$, and include all times necessary to perform the step with the respective method. Same applies for securing (t_{secure}), which we do not further subdivide, as activities necessary depend on the method used, and access to the unit needs to be considered in the respective values. Further, providing ($t_{provide}$) does not need to be subdivided, as the only significant parameter left is the way how the workplace is cleared: by pushing, putting or bending if the implementation is manual, and otherwise by the respective process time of the device. If a confirmation is necessary, time needed for this activity should be included in this value.

6.5 Item Time

In Section 6.1, we assigned the time shares for packing and checking to the item time. For packing, apart from the size of units, the second most important influencing parameter was the order of items. This factor might be not relevant if only one item is to be packed, items weigh approximately the same, are of the same stability, or the package or carrier is big enough. Else, it is required to reposition them. A similar reasoning applies for the type of items. If all articles are shaped in the same way, it is easier to position them, especially if the package or carrier is small. Even if they are of modular shape, figuring out how to position them requires less effort. For a variety of items, repositioning is more likely to be necessary.

Both parameters, order and type of items, can be included in the formula by using a 'repositioning factor' f_r, as for both the main effort needed is to reposition articles that have been placed already. This factor should be chosen according to the probability that articles need to be removed and placed again. As the factor is very unique for each system, the best way to determine the value is to measure it. Therefore, an analysis of the

6.5 Item Time

system, like work sampling, could be used. For details about this analysis we refer to Arnold and Furmans (2009, 248-250). The same factor can be used if more than one item are being grasped for packing at the same time. Consequently, f_r will be smaller than one in this case.

Times for picking up the items and placing them into or onto the shipping unit depend on the distance that the packer needs to reach and the weight and stability of goods. These influencing parameters have to be considered when determining the packing time by using one of the previously mentioned methods (cf. beginning of Section 6).

Additionally, we analysed the significance of a packing proposal. If a packing proposal is provided, there may not be a time share needed to find out where to put an article by trial and error, but time is necessary to find out where to put each item by studying the packing proposal. This time share has to be separated from the packing time, as it is not affected by repositioning.

Further, checking is part of the item time. In the analysis of Section 5.3, we found out that especially the type of checking is significant. So it needs to be a separate time share, and times need to be determined according to the respective method used. Time for confirmation has to be included with a share, according to the frequency in which it is being done compared to the checking frequency. Apart from this, checking might not be necessary for each item of the order and we use a factor f_s to be able to describe this sample size. Finally, several checks might be performed, like counting the amount and checking the identity, and therefore we need to sum up times.

The calculation of item time can be summarised as follows:

$$t_{item} = f_r \cdot t_{pack} + t_{proposal} + \sum f_s \cdot t_{check} \qquad (6.9)$$

All formulas given in Section 6, the basic structure as well as the detailed formulas, should be generally valid to calculate cycle times for packing. Intentionally, we did not consider the size of the units yet, as the idea was to use it to specify and classify formulas. In the following chapter (7), we want to identify these cases and validate the structure of the formulas of this Section (6) by refining them for the specific cases (cf. Sections 7.2

and 7.3). We also want to demonstrate the functionality performing proof of concepts and a case study of a specific case.

7 Validation

In this chapter, we want to identify a structure which can be used to refine packing in distribution centres. We build upon the results of the previous chapters for this purpose. At the same time, we want to select the most common cases for packing in distribution centres, to be able to validate the structure of the general formulas by applying and refining them for these cases in the following sections (cf. 7.2 and 7.3). Furthermore, we perform a case study on a very specific case to enhance the credibility in the general applicability of the formulas.

By validation "it has to be ensured that the model reflects the behaviour of the real system accurately enough and without error (Is it the right model for the task?)." (VDI 3633, 36) Further, VDI 3633 (36) states that the examination of the model needs to be problem-specific and an individual analysis regarding the targets is necessary. According to Rabe et al. (2008, 2), validating does not aim to provide a formal evidence of validity, but to attest the credibility of the model. Thereby, the credibility depends on the person who needs to 'accept' the results and thus a basis for this decision needs to be provided, which has to be as systematic as possible (Rabe et al. 2008, 3).

With regard to this, we want to validate the structure of the determined cycle time calculations. The system applied to examine the applicability of the structure is inspired by structural or white-box testing (cf. Balci 1998, 374): we evaluate cycle times based on their structure by identifying possible values for formula factors using common scenarios for packing in distribution centres. So according to testing the code coverage in the software development sector, we test whether each factor can be usefully covered for different cases typical for distribution centres. Therefore, we choose two scenarios which are different regarding the characteristic of unit handling (in other words, the two scenarios including the extreme values). To further analyse the generality, we perform a case study on a very specific packing job we observed in field.

So performing the white-box inspired testing method, we do not validate the functionality, but the structure of the identified formulas. Additionally, we perform a proof of concept for the two scenarios for the average case identified within a research project. This, as well as the case study, helps to improve the functional credibility of the formulas, but cannot be seen as validation of the functionality.

7.1 Derivation and Selection of Tasks for Validation

We summarised in Section 5.4 that dimensions of the handling units are important, especially if several of the process steps, like preparing the job, preparing the packaging, packing, checking, inserting add-in, securing, and providing the unit, are performed. But we also found out that it is not possible to model the size within a mathematical formula generally. In combination with the knowledge of process steps performed for packing (cf. Figure 4.2), we can derive tasks following Wisser and Hinding (2009), which can be distinguished and used to structure different cases of cycle times.

Tasks are defined by a particular state at the beginning and at the end of the operating activities. Both are defined in a way that the resulting effort is comparable. To distinguish tasks, different characteristics of the process and external requirements are considered (cf. Schwab, Weiblen and Furmans 2009, 313). At the same time, tasks are defined independently from the technical realisation, which is in line with the results of Section 5.4. There, dimensions showed to be more significant than the degree of automation throughout the whole analysis. This criterion could be used later on for further detailing.

For packing, we can distinguish which unit size is packed and which unit size results as a shipping unit to be able to define the start and final state. In order to distinguish different sizes and at the same time create a manageable amount of variations, we differentiate between pallets

7.1 Derivation and Selection of Tasks for Validation

or large load carriers (LLC), packages or small load carriers (SLC) as well as articles and mailing bags. We can derive the tasks P5 to P11 in Figure 7.1 by combining these unit sizes, and considering the process steps of Figure 4.2.

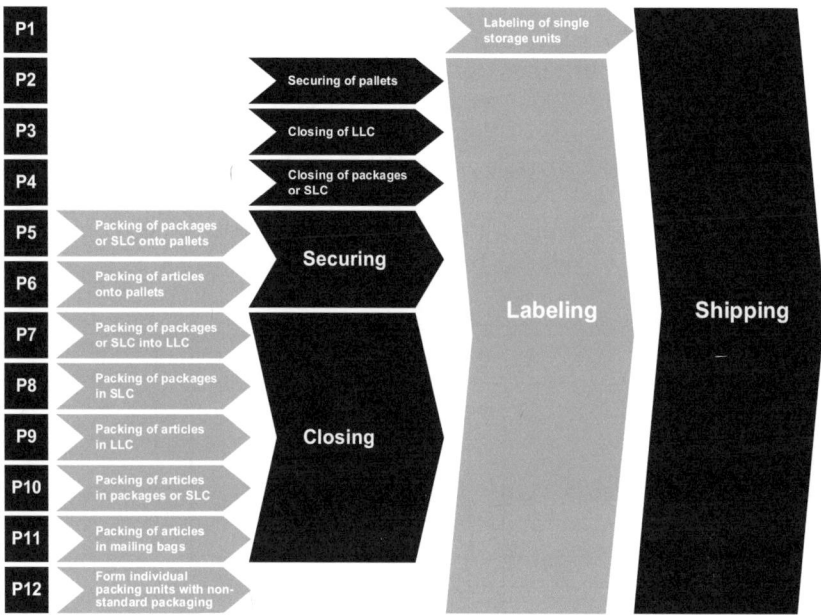

Figure 7.1: Packing tasks in distribution centres (Weiblen et al. 2012)

Sometimes no further packing process step is required for the customer, but the units are still secured and/or labelled for transport in the packing area. Further, we found out in Section 5.3 that especially securing depends on the dimensions of the handling unit. The different tasks resulting from these observations, no packing required and dependency on dimensions, are reflected in tasks P1 to P4.

Finally, we also need to define a task for the individual creation of a shipping unit if no standardised package is available, or standardised packages need to be adapted to the packing goods requirements. This task is represented by P12.

All these tasks can be used to structure packing in distribution centres. Since the most significant influencing parameter, the dimensions of the handling units, is used as a differentiating criterion, this design also helps to compare packing processes of different distribution centres in a benchmark.

We used the previously mentioned approach within a research project (Weiblen and Berbig 2011): we analysed 84 packing processes at 25 distribution centre locations in Europe, and categorised the areas according to the above mentioned task oriented approach. Figure 7.2 shows the distribution of the task incidence identified. We want to use these results to pick the two most common tasks and apply the formulas determined in Section 6 in order to validate the structure of the formulas.

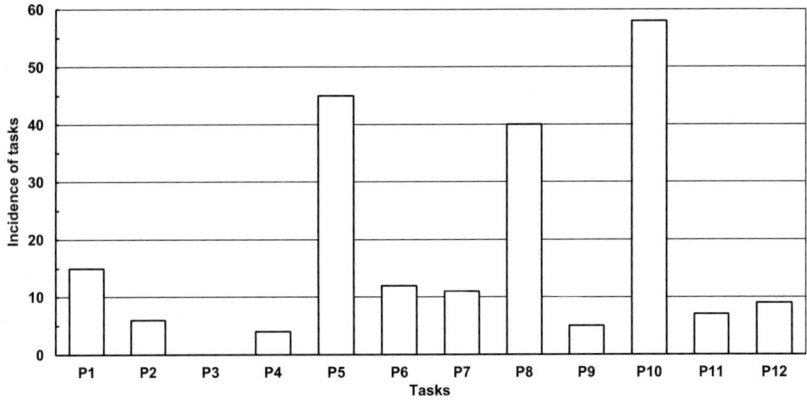

Figure 7.2: Incidence of tasks in distribution centres, n=212 (Weiblen and Berbig 2011)

We can observe that in 58 areas in distribution centres articles are packed in packages or small load carriers (P10). In 45 areas, these, other packages or small load carriers, are packed on pallets or large load carriers (P5). In 40 areas, packages are packed into packages or small load carriers (P8). The other tasks P1, P2, P4, P6, P7, P9, P11 and P12 are performed in between 4 and 15 areas, whereas P3 was not observed at all.

In the following, we want to investigate the two most common tasks: P10, the packing of articles in packages or small load carriers, and P5, the packing of packages or small load carriers on pallets. These two tasks already include the extreme values of the unit which is packed and the outgoing unit. We do not investigate task P8, the packing of packages into packages or small load carriers, separately as it is too similar to P10 for our purposes. For the other tasks, the data base would be too small to be able to perform also a proof of concept.

7.2 Packing Articles in Packages or Small Load Carriers

In this section, we take a closer look at the factors of the general cycle times for packing and their characteristics for the case that articles are packed into packages or small load carriers.

7.2.1 Travel Time

We start by having a look at the travel time. Usually, more than the items belonging to one shipping unit are transported at the same time, for example by using a trolley. We could hence use values for 'by foot (with trolley up to 40 kg)' from Table 6.1 for v and b, and assume a factor f_o of $\frac{1}{5}$, as we assume that 25 articles fit on one trolley and in median 5.6 articles belong to one shipping unit of P10 (Verpackungsprojekt 2011). In this example, we use a distance of $d = 5$ meters. To pick up and place the trolley we chose 1.3 s of the mentioned values for Formula 6.3.

Ready to be shipped units are usually also small, so several parcels or boxes can be transported at the same time. We use a trolley and assume a factor f_p of $\frac{1}{5}$ for transporting them together and use the respective values as above.

Usually, in the case under study, the packer does not leave his workplace towards a central area to accomplish activities. This is more common for securing of pallets which we will analyse in Section 7.3. As a result, the formula component $t_{t\_central}$ has to be set to zero for P10.

Inserting the mentioned values into the formulas of travel time (Formula 6.3 and 6.4), results in

$$t_{travel\_P10} = \frac{1}{5} \cdot (\frac{1.0}{1.3} + \frac{5.0}{1.0} + 1.3) + \frac{1}{5} \cdot (\frac{1.0}{1.3} + \frac{5.0}{1.0} + 1.3) + f_c \cdot 0 \qquad (7.1)$$
$$= 2.8 \; s$$

per outgoing shipping unit for transport operations. By applying the general formula to the task P10, we could show that the general Formula 6.4 for travel time is applicable and each factor can be covered for the task 'packing articles in packages or small load carriers'.

7.2.2 Set-up Time

If the IT-system is automated and information is being processed while the packer or the system works on the order, the time for information processing might not affect the cycle time of the system. On the other hand, if the packer or the system has to wait in the meantime, the time for information processing has to be measured or looked up in the system specifications. If system and packer work in parallel, we refer to our assumptions in Section 6 and use the longer value in order to calculate cycle time, while setting the other time to zero.

For partly automated or manual systems, times can be determined using the MTM methodology. These times depend on the respective system in place and should be analysed specifically. Considering a typical operation process for packing articles into packages or small load carriers we indicate values in Table 7.1 based on MTM. The detailed analysis and cases for which these times are applicable can be seen in Appendix A. Additionally, times such as for handling of the printed order (in case of handling 2.5 s) may apply.

By using MTM and modelling all components of the set-up time for typical implementations of 'packing articles in packages or small load carriers', we could show that in this case the Formula 6.5 is suitable.

7.2 Packing Articles in Packages or Small Load Carriers

Choosing job	automated/ not required [0 s]	pick randomly [1.8 s]	priority [2.5 s]	specified job [6.7 s]
Confirmation on start	automated/ not required [0 s]	manual/ automated [2.2 s]	manual input [3.2 s]	manual [3.4 s]
Identification	automated/ not required [0 s]	manual/ automated [2.2 s]	manual comparison [2.3 s]	
Decision on packaging	provided proposal [0.9 s]	standard [2.2 s]	packer's decision [6.5 s]	
Decision on protection material	not required [0 s]	provided proposal [0.9 s]	standard [2.2 s]	packer's decision [6.5 s]
Decision on securing method	provided proposal [0.9 s]	standard [2.2 s]	packer's decision [6.5 s]	
Initialisation print	automated/ not required [0 s]	manual / automated [2.2 s]	manual input [3.2 s]	
Marking (manual)	self adhesive [2.3 s]	glueing [6.8 s]	signing [19.6 s]	

Table 7.1: Typical values for set-up times for P10 using MTM

7.2.3 Base Time

For the base time as well, we want to explore if the formulas determined in Section 6.4 are suitable for 'packing articles in packages or small load carriers' and if each factor is covered.

For preparing the packaging, we first need to set up the packaging. For manual processes we can determine MTM times. Depending on the size, MTM-SVL offers three different values for FEFCO 02 types (FEFCO 2007), for taking the packaging, positioning, setting up and closing: for packages smaller than 30x30x30 cm: 7.7 s, 50x50x50 cm: 12.1 s and

80x80x80 cm: 16.0 s. We realise that, apart from fixing the joints and assembling, all components included in Formula 6.7 are already included in these MTM-SVL values. But of course it is possible to calculate separate values using a lower MTM aggregation level. For fixing the joints by taping less than 30 cm, 4.0 s are indicated, for 50 cm 5.2 s, and for 80 cm 6.1 s. Closing an additional flap is calculated with 1.3 s. As mentioned earlier, assembling a loading should only occur in P12, so here regarding P10 we set this factor equal to zero.

For protecting, we found out that the used material has an impact, especially if the operation is performed manually. Materials for filling the hollow vary a lot, and in MTM there are no given values. Consequently, processes have to be analysed individually, and times, such as for 'pouring' of MTM-SVL, which can be used for loose/liquid protection material, have to be chosen accordingly.

If an add-in is inserted into or onto a package, the size of it within this task should not exceed limits where a special device is necessary for handling. Basically, we should have small add-ins that need to be put into or onto the package. For manual systems, MTM-SVL indicates values between 1.8 s to 2.0 s to transfer a single, not bulky item inside the package. If it is a piece of paper, like a receipt, 2.5 s are given. If for instance the provision is out of reach and the packer needs to bend in order to grasp the add-ins, another 2.2 s for each bending are necessary. Putting an add-in onto a unit or putting it into a messenger bag before inserting needs to be analysed individually according to the system in place using MTM-1, for instance. For attaching a receipt to the package from outside, we used the time of 4.0 s analysed for this purpose in Dzeik and Picker (2003). As we have seen in Table 5.18, also initializing the print and folding are significant. The time required to initialise the print, depends a lot on the system in place, and whether the packer needs to type the order number, just clicks or pushes a button to start printing. But as a reference, times given in Table 7.1 can be used. If the receipt is folded, time has to be calculated accordingly. We analysed 3.6 s for the analysis of variance. All activities listed in Formula 6.8 can be found for 'packing articles in packages or small load carriers'. If, for example, two giveaways and one receipt have to be added, we need to sum up 1.8 s, 1.8 s and 2.5 s for inserting the already printed receipt. In total, 6.1 s are necessary, and the fact of summing up multiple and different kinds of add-ins is considered in Formula 6.6.

7.2 Packing Articles in Packages or Small Load Carriers

For securing, also the degree of automation needs to be considered, as mentioned before. When securing a parcel, usually the package or small load carrier needs to be closed and joints need to be fixed. For the FEFCO 02 types (FEFCO 2007), times for closing are included in the values given for set up within 'prepare packaging' and therefore in the base time. We also indicated times for fixing the joints by taping there (cf. Section 7.2.3). Additionally, packages sometimes need to be strapped if they exceed a certain weight limit for instance. For manual strapping of one strap (not depending on the size) MTM-SVL indicates 43.2 s, 20.7 s if an electrical device is used, and for a stationary machine 5.6 s are assumed. Within the research project (Verpackungsprojekt 2011), we did not find shrink or stretch wrapping in combination with this task of 'packing articles into packages or small load carrier' (P10). Nevertheless, if this combination is employed, times need to be analysed accordingly. Otherwise, we found packing processes, where it is necessary to close small load carrier. This is included in the sub-process 'secure' as we defined in Chapter 4. For closing a lid, MTM-SVL indicates between 2.2 and 4.1 s depending on the size.

If the packing is carried out manually and even if the transport of shipping units to the next area is automated, the units need to be provided somehow. This might be by pushing units onto a conveyor. MTM-SVL does not give a specific value for pushing, but we analysed it with a duration of 0.9 s for the analysis of Section 5.3.3. For putting the package or small loading carrier onto a conveyor or trolley, MTM-SVL differs between small (smaller than 30x30x30 cm) and big (bigger than 30x30x30 cm) units, and specifies 3.2 and 4.5 s, respectively. Additional 2.2 s are necessary for bending. All given values refer to a distance of up to 80 cm. If the workplace is very tiny, times might be shorter than indicated. If it is bigger, additional times might apply for moving if not everything is in reach of the packer, which needs to be analysed separately as well.

We have seen that for the single components of the base time (Formula 6.7 and 6.8) as well as the complete calculation (Formula 6.6), all components can be specified for 'packing articles in packages or small load carriers' and therefore validated their structure using this example.

7.2.4 Item Time

Grasping articles depends a lot on influencing parameters. We found out in Section 5.3 that especially the size of the unit has an influence. We took account of this fact by differentiating the tasks. In this section, we only focus on articles that need to be put in packages or small load carriers and assume average values for articles within one shipping unit.

Values for reaching for the article, picking it up and placing it according to MTM-UAS, and depending on the influencing parameters, are given in Table 7.2.

Weight	Stability	Distance	
		20-50cm	50-80cm
<=1kg	stable	1.3 s	1.8 s
	flexible/fragile	1.6 s	2.2 s
1-8kg	stable	1.6 s	2.0 s
	flexible/fragile	2.3 s	2.7 s
8-22kg	stable	3.8 s	4.1 s
	flexible/fragile	4.3 s	4.7 s

Table 7.2: Typical times for packing single units following MTM-UAS

Other technical implementations can hardly be found in distribution centres, as items are difficult to be grasped automatically. For automated systems, usually there must be a packing proposal to enable the machine to place the articles correctly. Most likely, articles are already in the right order, or are grasped according to given requirements. Times vary along with variety and stability of items as well, and need to be determined using the respective manufacturer specifications.

As mentioned in Section 6.5, the factor for repositioning has to be determined individually. In many systems certain times are necessary to reposition articles that are not in the right order, but it is very uncommon that one has to reposition them due to a packing proposal (only 21 percent of all areas use proposals, cf. Verpackungsprojekt 2011).

In Formula 6.9, we also distinguished one time component to consider the packing proposal. This time can be approximated by the MTM-SVL time of 'comparing a code' with 1.6 seconds per article.

The most common check after amount is on identity, which is also backed up by results of the research project (Weiblen and Berbig 2011). Comparing codes without a device can be derived from MTM-SVL with 1.6 s. This assumes that checking and packing are performed in parallel and items are already grasped. Times for picking up units need to be analysed separately if these processes are not combined. Also additional times, like picking up a list (2.5 s) or turning the unit, need to be analysed separately. If using a scanner for the identity check, MTM-SVL indicates 2.2 s. If the input needs to be given manually, 0.9 s are necessary for pressing a single button, but a code might have to be compared as well (another 1.6 s). The same applies when every item needs to be signed manually on a list. Then signing requires 1.4 s.

The other types of checking are too special to be able to generalise them. For automated systems, it depends whether the process time of the automated system affects the overall system time or not. If the cycle time for an automated system has to be calculated, the process time needs to be considered. On the other hand, if the cycle time is calculated for a manual process, and the packer does not need to wait for the automated processes, the cycle time is not affected by the automated process activities. In that case, the time for checking would be zero.

As a result, all components of the item time are useful to calculate packing time for 'packing articles in packages or small load carriers'.

7.2.5 Proof of Concept

Within the previous sections, we intended to verify the applicability of the general formulas derived in Section 6.1 to the task of 'packing articles in packages or small load carriers' and therefore enhance the credibility of these formulas. Summing up the results, we can state that all components of the basic formula, namely travel, set-up, base and item times as well as the components of the refined formulas can be instantiated and used for this purpose. So we were able to validate the structure using this task.

Going one step further, we can compare the values for this task indicated in the previous sections with empirical data from the research project (Verpackungsprojekt 2011) in order to investigate the functionality. Therefore, we analyse the available information on activities and characteristics of the task 'packing articles in packages or small load carriers'. This helps us to derive the average realisation of this task based on values of 58 packing processes.

Of cause, using an average case and using historical data comprises several problems: information on the processing of the task is limited but is a given, and for missing information assumptions have to be made. The quality of the data can be doubted for this detailing level at least partly, especially when taking a close look on time values per shipping unit. Distribution centres indicated values for performing the task for all units per day and most likely also included time shares for secondary supply, technical downtimes, unproductive times and usability like waiting times for instance. We cannot quantify these time shares as they are too individual. Using an average case of cause leads to variation within the process, which leads to problems with variances, especially for a small number of observations. But still, we want to use the average case to enhance the functional credibility of the formulas and to give a hint how realistic the calculated values are, or what needs to be considered when investigate cases using the formulas.

In average, items and packages are not supplied or provided by the packer as conveyors are used in 62 percent of the cases for the supply with items and in 46 percent for the provision of the shipping unit. The packer also does not leave his workplace for a central area. Therefore, travel time can be set to zero.

Regarding the set-up time, we partly need to assume what the packer needs to do, as for other time components as well, because we use historical data and the process description is not detailed enough. So we assume that he does not need to choose the next job, as items are provided with a conveyor. Additionally, we assume that the confirmation on start is given with the first scan of an item, which is also used to identify the packing job, so no additional time is necessary. We know that he needs to decide on the packaging (6.5 s), as 80 percent of the packing processes do not provide packaging proposals. 70 percent of the areas use protection material which is made of paper, so we presume that no decision on this is necessary. In most of the cases, no decision on securing is required either, as 96 percent of the areas only fix the joints. In 88 percent of the cases, marking is necessary, but only once, as only 16 percent use additional labels. We assume that printing labels starts automatically and add only 2.3 s for the activity of labelling. In total, we can calculate the set-up time as follows:

$$\begin{aligned} t_{set\text{-}up} &= t_{choose} + t_{confirm} + t_{identify} + t_{d\_packaging} \\ &\quad + t_{d\_protect} + t_{d\_secure} + t_{print} + \sum t_{mark} \\ &= 0\ s + 0\ s + 0\ s + 6.5\ s + 0\ s + 0\ s + 0\ s + 2.3\ s \\ &= 8.8\ s \end{aligned} \quad (7.2)$$

The base time includes the preparing of the packaging. We discovered that MTM-SVL summarises the actions taking, positioning, setting up and closing of the packaging in Section 7.2.3. The average size of the package in the areas is 40x35x35 cm and therefore 12.1 s are needed. To fix the first joint additional 5.2 s are necessary. We learned that for protection mainly paper is used, which needs to be analysed specifically. For the analysis of variance in Section 5.3.3, we determined preparing the protection paper and inserting it with 19.1 s. As type of add-in, the majority of the packing processes (68 percent) only insert the delivery note (2.5 s). We assume that it does not need to be folded. A further assumption is that the packer needs to manually confirm the printing of the delivery note, which takes 3.2 s. We mentioned that packages are secured by fixing the joint, so we add another 5.2 s for this purpose. For providing the package we assume that the packer has to put it on the conveyor, which takes 4.5 s. In total, we end up at a base time of 51.8 s for this task:

$$\begin{aligned} t_{base} &= t_{prepare} + t_{protect} + \sum t_{add\text{-}in} + \sum t_{secure} + t_{provide} \\ &= (12.1 + 5.2)\ s + 19.1\ s + (2.5 + 3.2)\ s + 5.2\ s + 4.5\ s \\ &= 51.8\ s \end{aligned} \quad (7.3)$$

Looking at the item time, we need to multiply values for packing and checking with the average of 5.6 articles per package, as they are checked completely. The weight of an article is 1.8 kg and consequently, 2.0 s are necessary to pack each article. No factor for repositioning is given and we assume it to be one. Only 2 percent of the areas use a packing proposal, so in our case no time is needed for studying the proposal. 67 percent of the areas check both, amount and identity, mainly by scanning every item. We assume that both criteria are checked in the course of this activity, which results in 2.2 s for the scanning. In summary we calculate the item time as follows:

$$
\begin{aligned}
t_{item} &= f_r \cdot t_{pack} + t_{proposal} + \sum f_s \cdot t_{check} \\
&= 1 \cdot 2.0 \ s + 0 \ s + 1 \cdot 2.2 \ s \\
&= 4.2 \ s
\end{aligned}
\tag{7.4}
$$

As mentioned, several times, additional movements like turning or stepping forward, may apply together with another movement. In the research project (Verpackungsprojekt 2011), we observed that in average a packer needs to do nine steps during the packing process of this task. According to MTM-SVL, this means to add another 5.4 s. We also found out that the radius of movement while packing is bigger than 180°, which means that the packer turns round and back again at least once while performing the packing task. Therefore, another 1.2 s apply. This is a best case assumption, because we do not have data on how often a packer really turns around. Usually one would analyse this with the respective activity, but we do not know in combination with which activity they accrue, so we add them separately here.

All in all, we calculate the packing time as follows:

$$
\begin{aligned}
t_{packing} &= t_{travel} + t_{set\text{-}up} + t_{base} + n \cdot t_{item} \\
&= 0 \ s + 8.8 \ s + 51.8 \ s + 5.6 \cdot 4.2 \ s + 5.4 \ s + 1.2 \ s \\
&= 90.7 \ s
\end{aligned}
\tag{7.5}
$$

As mentioned at the beginning of Chapter 6, this does not include a factor for availability and usability. According to Dangelmaier (2001, 490), six to 15 percent need to be added to the calculated packing time for allowances as well as five to ten percent for recreation, which both relate to the availability. Taking this into account we end up at 114.8 s per package, but we still did not consider technical downtimes, unproductive times and non-packing related secondary work as well as usability. The median for this packing task in the research project data (Verpackungsprojekt 2011) is 332.6 s with a total range of 6.9 to 6776.5 s and a standard deviation of 1685 s (based on data of 17 areas, which share the same average realisation than the 58 areas). These times also include all additional time shares which are impossible for us to quantify, and movements which we did not analyse, because the available data was not detailed enough.

In other words, we showed in Section 7.2 that the cycle time factors are covered for the task 'packing articles in packages or small load carriers', and therefore the structure can be validated using this case. Times derived for an average case are realistic and served to enhance the functional credibility of the formulas.

7.3 Packing Packages or Small Load Carriers on Pallets

In Section 7.1, we have seen that 'packing packages or small load carriers on pallets' is the second most important task of packing in distribution centres and covers the other extreme dimensions of incoming and outgoing units. In the following, we want to find out if we can use the general cycle time formulas determined in Section 6 for this task as well.

7.3.1 Travel Time

For 'packing of packages or small load carriers on pallets', the packer usually needs to travel some distances while packing. As mentioned before, especially securing devices for pallets are often located in a central area and shared by several packers. Therefore, the term $t_{t\_central}$ is more likely to be used. It is calculated as given in Formula 6.3, and we need to consider the distance, velocity and acceleration, where the last two can be looked up using 'by foot (with powered trolley up to 1500 kg)' of Table 6.1, as usually pallet jacks assist for transportation. Picking up and placing with pallet jacks was indicated with 12.6 to 22.1 s in Section 6.2.

In this case, items are typically bigger than in the previous one, as we have packages or small loads compared to articles in the section before. We still can transport more items than for one shipping unit at the same time, again by using a trolley. But it is more likely that one trolley is for one shipping unit only, as the volume of items is higher and the volume of a pallet needs to be filled. In median 17.4 packages are on one pallet (Verpackungsprojekt 2011). So we can use values given for 'by foot (with trolley up to 40 kg)' or for higher weights 'by foot (with powered trolley up to 1500 kg)' from Table 6.1 and assume a factor of $f_o = 1$, for example. If volumes of items are higher, maybe even two or more trolleys per pallet are necessary, resulting in a factor of $f_o > 2$.

Pallets that are ready to be shipped are usually transported using a pallet jack. Consequently, the travel time for providing can be calculated again with 'by foot (with powered trolley up to 1500 kg)', and usually one pallet at a time will be transported. So the factor f_p equals 1. Besides, for supplying and providing we need to consider the duration of pick up and placing with the pallet jack or trolley.

As we can see, all components of Formula 6.4 can be specified and are useful for the task of 'packing packages or small load carriers on pallets'.

7.3.2 Set-up Time

As for 'packing articles in packages or small load carriers', also for 'packing packages or small load carriers on pallets' we have to think about times, which are related to information processing, and which do not obviously change the condition of the shipping unit. In general, these times related to information processing will be very similar to the ones for articles, but the bigger dimensions of the units, as well as the more standardised character of outgoing units lead to slight changes. Reference values, which are related to the activities described in Appendix B, are given in Table 7.3.

We can see that we only have to change the values given in Table 7.3 in comparison to Table 7.1, which would also be necessary if focusing on more automated systems. Therefore, we were able to show that Formula 6.5 is applicable for this task (P5) as well and that again all components are covered.

7.3 Packing Packages or Small Load Carriers on Pallets

Choosing job	automated/ not required [0 s]	pick randomly [2.5 s]	priority [4.0 s]	specified job [8.5 s]	
Confirmation on start	automated/ not required [0 s]	manual/ automated [3.1 s]	manual input [4.1 s]	manual [4.3 s]	
Identification	automated/ not required [0 s]	manual/ automated [3.1 s]	manual comparison [3.1 s]		
Decision on packaging	provided proposal [0.9 s]	standard [1.1 s]	packer's decision [3.2 s]		
Decision on protection material	not required [0 s]	provided proposal [0.9 s]	standard [1.1 s]	packer's decision [5.4 s]	
Decision on securing method	provided proposal [0.9 s]	standard [2.2 s]	packer's decision [6.5 s]		
Initialisation print	automated/ not required [0 s]	manual / automated [3.1 s]	manual input [4.1 s]		
Marking (manual)	self adhesive [3.2 s]	glueing [7.7 s]	signing [20.5 s]		

Table 7.3: Typical values for set-up times for P5 using MTM

7.3.3 Base Time

For packing pallets, base times depend a lot on the respective system in place. In the following, we indicate some values which give an idea about respective times, but systems need to be analysed individually.

The preparing of a pallet usually includes only the setting up and positioning of the pallet, and neither fixing the joint nor opening or assembling the unit. Setting up the pallet refers to putting it into place, which MTM-SVL specifies for the manual process with 7.6 s.

Protecting is rarely used in combination with packing of pallets. If protecting is necessary, the manual activities have to be analysed using MTM individually.

If an add-in is added to a pallet, the size of it might vary. We discussed receipts and smaller items in Section 7.2, and those values apply for pallets as well. But required movements like turning or side steps might be necessary, which need to be analysed additionally. For packing add-ins onto a pallet, a special device, like a crane, might be necessary. No general values can be given, but times need to be analysed individually using MTM-SVL, for instance.

In addition, for securing of pallets, the degree of automation needs to be considered. Pallets usually do not need to be closed, but are strapped, shrink or stretch wrapped. As mentioned before, MTM-SVL does not differ between sizes for strapping, so the same time values as given in Section 7.2.3 for packages apply. A value for stretching a pallet with the help of a machine is specified as well with 62.3 s. Thereby, the foil has to be attached to the pallet manually, the button has to be pressed, and eventually the foil has to be adjusted. The time is calculated for six windings and needs to be adapted accordingly. For a completely manual process, where the packer walks around the pallet, we analysed 105.9 s, which includes eight windings. For shrinking a pallet no values are given in MTM methods, but it can be analysed individually. For the analysis described in Section 5.3 and shrinking being done completely manual, we calculated 107.9 s. Some of the authors mentioned in Chapter 2 and 4 also indicate values for the different techniques. These values are provided on an hourly or daily (we assumed eight hours) basis and it is not indicated whether availability is included or not. If we determine the time per pallet in seconds, we get the following results: for strapping values between 240 s (manual) and 30 s (automated) (Arnold et al. 2008, 708), for stretching 30 s (automated) (VDI 3968-5 2009), and for shrinking 576 s (manual) to 24 s (automated) (Arnold et al. 2008, 710). If a wire mesh box needs to be closed, 4.1 s per lid can be assumed according to MTM-SVL.

Also pallets need to be provided somehow. Pallets usually cannot be pushed or carried, but have to be put onto a conveyor using a pallet jack or a fork lift. MTM-SVL differs between the weight of a pallet and if the pallet needs to be positioned. For less than 500 kg, 29.3 s with adjusting the position and 17.1 s without are indicated. For more than 500 kg, 33.3 and 19.6 s are given respectively. Additional movements have to be analysed separately, as times only include the lifting and the placing of the pallet using a pallet jack. For a sit-on fork lift, to lift the pallet up and down, MTM-SVL indicates 30.0 s with, and 21.7 s without rotating the pallet by 90°. If the unit has to be transported further to a provision area, we do not need to analyse provision separately, as the picking up is already included in the travel time.

Again, we showed that for 'packing packages or small load carriers on pallets' all components of formulas in Section 6.4 are useful to be able to calculate the time required.

7.3.4 Item Time

Like in Section 7.2.4 for articles, packages or small load carriers might need to be repositioned because they are provided in the wrong order, or they are of different shape and need to be repositioned to achieve stability of the loading unit. The second case is more likely for this task than for the smaller units, since stability has to be provided by stacking, because usually no protection material is used. As a result, the factor for repositioning (f_r) needs to be distinguished according to the given circumstances.

Also the time for picking up a unit and placing it can be analysed according to Table 7.2, but times have to be added to take into account the larger movements: for example for bending (2.2 s, MTM-SVL), walking (0.9 s/m, MTM-SVL) and turning (0.7 s/90°, MTM-1).

The time required to study the packing proposal does not differ from values given in Section 7.2.4, and time for checking is similar as well. However, in addition to the times for checking given before, the times mentioned in this section for additional movements or times for eye travelling need to be considered, as workplaces for pallets are bigger than for small loads.

For this task, we could quantify all components determined in Section 6.5 to calculate item time. Also for the other time components included in Formula 6.2 the we covered all components for the case 'packing packages or small load carriers on pallets'. Therefore, we were able to validate the general formula with this case as well.

7.3.5 Proof of Concept

Here again, for the task of 'packing packages or small load carriers on pallets', we demonstrated the applicability of the general formulas determined in Section 6 and, again, we want to go one step further, consider the functionality and compare values with empirical data from the research project (Verpackungsprojekt 2011). This time, we derive the average realisation of this task based on data of 45 packing processes and again we have to be aware of the problems comprised with this approach (cf. Section 7.2.5).

Packages are not supplied by the packer as conveyors are used in 58 percent of the cases. But this time, the packer leaves his workplace for a central area to be able to stretch wrap the pallet. Further, he provides the pallet manually using a pallet jack in 47 percent of the cases. We do not have data on distances, but assume that the central area for stretching is 10 meters and the provision area is 20 meters away from the packing area. Another assumption is that each pallet is transported separately. We calculate the travel time as follows:

$$\begin{aligned} t_{travel} &= f_o \cdot t_{t\_supply} + f_p \cdot t_{t\_provide} + f_c \cdot t_{t\_central} \\ &= 0 \; s + 1 \cdot (\frac{1.3}{0.8} + \frac{2 \cdot 20}{1.3} + 18.7 + 10.6) \; s \\ &+ 1 \cdot (\frac{1.3}{0.8} + \frac{2 \cdot 10}{1.3} + 18.7 + 10.6) \; s \\ &= 108.0 \; s \end{aligned} \quad (7.6)$$

Here as well, we partly need to assume what the packer has to do in order to calculate for example the set-up time, as we do not have complete process descriptions. We assume that he does not need to choose the next job, as items are provided with the conveyor. In addition, we take for granted that no confirmation on start is necessary, and he needs to identify the packing job by manual comparison, which takes 3.1 s. We assume that no decision on packaging, on protection or on securing is necessary. In 64

7.3 Packing Packages or Small Load Carriers on Pallets

percent of the cases marking is necessary, but mostly only once as only 22 percent have additional labels. This activity takes 3.2 s. We assume that the packer needs to start the printing of the label with a manual input which takes him 4.1 s. In total, we can calculate the set-up time as follows:

$$\begin{aligned} t_{set\text{-}up} &= t_{choose} + t_{confirm} + t_{identify} + t_{d\_packaging} \\ &\quad + t_{d\_protect} + t_{d\_secure} + t_{print} + \sum t_{mark} \\ &= 0\ s + 0\ s + 3.1\ s + 0\ s + 0\ s + 0\ s + 4.1\ s + 3.2\ s \\ &= 10.4\ s \end{aligned} \quad (7.7)$$

The base time includes activities for preparing the packaging, which in this case are for setting up the pallet and for its positioning. According to MTM-SVL this takes 7.6 s. In 53 percent of the research project cases no protection material is necessary, but we need to consider that we only have data on time from nine areas. There, crumbled paper is added for protection. As we do not have details on the quantity and the activities, we assume that the packer needs to do a minimum of seven steps to get to the material provision, to step back when tearing it off and to walk around the pallet for positioning it. Of cause, he also needs to tear the paper and crumple it and analysing it analogue to Chapter 5 results in 20.0 s in total. The majority of the packing processes (71 percent) only insert a delivery note (2.5 s) as an add-in, which we assume has not to be folded. A further assumption is that the packer needs to confirm the printing of the delivery note manually, which takes 3.2 s. The pallet is secured in 64 percent of the areas by stretching it semi-automated, which is indicated with 62.3 s in MTM-SVL. The picking up of the pallet and putting it down for provision is already included in the travel time and is zero here. In total we arrive at a base time of 95.6 s:

$$\begin{aligned} t_{base} &= t_{prepare} + t_{protect} + \sum t_{add\text{-}in} + \sum t_{secure} + t_{provide} \\ &= 7.6\ s + 20.0\ s + (2.5 + 3.2)\ s + 62.3\ s + 0\ s \\ &= 95.6\ s \end{aligned} \quad (7.8)$$

For this task, we need to multiply values for packing and checking with the 17.4 packages which are compiled in average on one pallet. The average weight of an article is 13 kg and, therefore, 4.1 s are necessary to pack each article. Additionally, as packing workplaces were not designed very ergonomically, the packer needs to bend (2.2 s) and to turn each time, as in 57 percent of the areas the radius for the packer is bigger than 270°. In this case, we set the factor for repositioning to 1.2 which means that in 20 percent of the cases he needs to adjust the position of the packages. Only 3 percent of the areas use a packing proposal, so no time is necessary for studying a proposal. 70 percent of the areas manually check both, amount and identity, and every package is checked individually. We assume that both criteria are checked in parallel and each package is checked by the packer on a list. This results in 1.6 s for comparing the code, 1.4 s for checking on the list and 2.5 s for handling the list. In summary we can calculate the item time as follows:

$$\begin{aligned} t_{item} &= f_r \cdot t_{pack} + t_{proposal} + \sum f_s \cdot t_{check} \\ &= 1.2 \cdot (4.1 + 2.2 + 4 \cdot 0.6)\ s + 0\ s + 1 \cdot (1.6 + 1.4 + 2.5)\ s \\ &= 15.9\ s \end{aligned} \quad (7.9)$$

Additional movements like turning or stepping forward may apply combined with another movement. In the research project (Verpackungsprojekt 2011) we identified that in average a packer needs to do 18 steps during the packing process of this task. Using MTM-SVL, this adds another 10.8 s. As already mentioned, the radius is usually larger than 270° in most of the cases. We already considered this for packing but at least for activities associated with the delivery note there will be another 2.4 s which we add separately.

To summarise we calculate the packing time as follows:

$$\begin{aligned} t_{packing} &= t_{travel} + t_{set\text{-}up} + t_{base} + n \cdot t_{item} \\ &= 108.0\ s + 10.4\ s + 95.6\ s + 17.4 \cdot 15.9\ s + 10.8\ s + 2.4\ s \\ &= 503.9\ s \end{aligned}$$

$$(7.10)$$

If we multiply this time with the factor for allowances and recreation (cf. Section 7.2.5), we end up with 637 s per pallet. The median for this packing task in the research project data (Verpackungsprojekt 2011) is 2880 s or

48 minutes with a range from the minimum of 720 s to the maximum of 7982 s and a standard deviation of 2434 s. As mentioned, for this task nine areas provided us performance data. Here again, times provided by the distribution centres include technical downtimes, unproductive times and non-packing related secondary work as well as usability, which we could not consider in our calculation. For this task, we realise the problems mentioned in Section 7.2.5 with the chosen approach: More than two hours for packing one pallet seems to be unrealistic and the data quality must be questioned. Additionally, also for this task we had to make assumptions as we did not have a detailed process description and used best-case assumptions where possible. Further, we can anticipate that a lot more additional movements like bending and turning are necessary, which we assumed to be at a minimum. This reasons lead to a lower calculated cycle time compared to the empirical values available. As a consequence for planning, additional times are necessary to be quantified and planners have to be aware that if no additional movements are analysed times are rather underestimated.

For the task 'packing packages or small load carriers on pallets', we quantified the elements of the cycle time calculation in Section 7.3 successfully, and therefore validated the structure of the formulas. The times determined in the proof of concept seem to be reasonable, but are not in the range indicated by the data of the research project (Verpackungsprojekt 2011). Reasons for this might be that we did not quantify some of the additional times in our calculation, which are included in the data of industry partners, that the data might not be reliable and that assumptions had to be made.

7.4 Case Study

In Chapter 6, we determined formulas to calculate cycle times for packing in distribution centres. We then demonstrated the applicability of these formulas for the two most common cases in this chapter. We found out that these two cases can be modelled and calculated using the determined formulas, even though the two cases are very different, as one refers to small loads and the other one to pallets as shipping units (cf. Sections 7.2

and 7.3). One can hence argue that naturally the most common cases can be modelled using these formulas.

To enhance the credibility in the generality of the formulas in the following, we want to have a look at an implemented, very specific packing area which we visited within the research project on packing. It has been designated as task P12 (cf. Figure 7.1, Verpackungsprojekt 2011). The job was to pack a varying amount of chairs and/or other furniture for shipping. For this purpose, big loading units were built using a pallet and corrugated cardboard, which was cut and fixed according to the shape and height necessary. Further, the amount and identity of the products were checked manually and a delivery note was inserted. Crumpled paper was used to fill voids, and after packing the unit was secured by strapping and stretching. Before providing the unit for the shipping area, it was also marked. Packers needed to transport in order to fetch the chairs as well as for stretching and finally for providing the units.

We start by analysing the travel time: For t_{t_supply} the packer needs to fetch the chairs with a pallet jack, where he might need to travel several times, but we anticipate that f_o is one. Consequently, we can use values given by Table 6.1. The single distance between the provision area and the packing area is 50 meters. Weight is more than 500 kg and we need to add time for picking up (14,9 s, MTM-SVL), and later on placing (11.2 s, MTM-SVL). Then, we need to calculate the travel time to reach the securing area. Each pallet or unit has to be transported separately, therefore f_c equals one. The single distance was about ten meters and items were transported on a pallet jack, so same figures apply here than for supply. Also for provision we can use the same figures. Here again, the single distance is 50 meters. There are differences in picking up, which has to be done including adjustments in position (22.1 s, MTM-SVL) and in placing, which can be done without adjustments (4.7 s, MTM-SVL). In all, we can calculate travel time as follows:

7.4 Case Study

$$\begin{aligned}
t_{C1\_travel} &= 1 \cdot (\frac{1.3}{0.8} + \frac{100}{1.3} + 14.9 + 11.2) \ s \\
&+ 1 \cdot (\frac{1.3}{0.8} + \frac{20}{1.3} + 14.9 + 11.2) \ s \\
&+ 1 \cdot (\frac{1.3}{0.8} + \frac{100}{1.3} + 22.1 + 4.7) \ s \\
&= 253.1 \ s
\end{aligned} \qquad (7.11)$$

We then proceed with calculating the set-up time. The packer needs to choose the next job, which is given, so 8.5 s are necessary (cf. Table 7.3). To confirm the start, he scans the order ($t_{confirm} = 3.1 \ s$, Table 7.3). Therefore and for identifying, he picks the delivery note. To get the time for identification, we need to add 3.1 s and 2.5 s for picking up and putting down the delivery note (cf. Table 7.3). Based on the information obtained, he decides on packaging, protection and securing, for which we use the respective values given in Table 7.3. He does not need to print the label, as it is attached to the delivery note, so for marking he simply takes the label (2.5 s) and attaches it to the unit (3.2 s, Table 7.3).

$$\begin{aligned}
t_{C1\_set\text{-}up} &= 8.5 \ s + 3.1 \ s + (3.1 + 2.5) \ s + 3.2 \ s + 5.4 \ s \\
&+ 6.5 \ s + 0 \ s + (3.2 + 2.5) \ s \\
&= 38.0 \ s
\end{aligned} \qquad (7.12)$$

The next time to calculate is the base time. For preparing, the pallet needs to be set up, then the corrugated cardboard needs to be cut, which is part of assembling, and finally the cardboard is fixed by taping. The packer does not need to position or open the unit. For cutting the corrugated cardboard, we can sum up the positioning of the scissor on the corrugated cardboard (MTM-SD 2.3 s) and cutting (MTM-SD 15x 0.2). This has to be done on two sides of each corrugated cardboard and for five corrugated cardboards in total (four for each side of the pallet, and one for the top). In between, the packer also needs to replace the cut cardboard (MTM-SVL 2.0 s). Then, he needs to position the cut board around the furniture (MTM-SVL: walking once around the pallet 1.8 s, replacing the cardboard each 2.0 s) and finally fix the joints. Fixing the joints is being done by picking up the tape dispenser (MTM-SVL 2.0 s), and applying two horizontal strips for each corner and two vertical ones for the top (MTM-SVL each strip 5.2 s). In order to be able to do this, again the packer needs to walk around the pallet (MTM-SVL 1.8 s).

$$\begin{aligned} t_{C1\_prepare} &= 7.6\ s + ((2 + 4 \cdot 2) \cdot 5.2\ s + 2.0\ s + 1.8\ s) \\ &+ (2 \cdot 5 \cdot (2.3 + 3.0)\ s + 5 \cdot 2.0\ s + 1.8\ s + 5 \cdot 2.0\ s) \\ &+ 0\ s + 0\ s \\ &= 138.2\ s \end{aligned} \quad (7.13)$$

For protecting, crumpled paper is needed. Therefore, the packer takes a pre-cut piece of paper and crumples it, before he can place it between the furniture. Of course, the quantity used varies, but we observed that it this is necessary for half of the chairs, so 18 times. Picking up the sheet and placing it can be analysed with 2.1 s (MTM-SD). In between, the sheet needs to be crumpled, which we analyse with three times 1.6 s (MTM-1). If we sum up these values and multiply them with 18, it results in 124.2 s. Here as well, he needs to move around the pallet (MTM-SVL 1.8 s). So, we get to 126.0 s for protecting the unit, in total.

We also need to analyse the time to insert the delivery note. As mentioned, the delivery note has already been printed and is just put on top of the stacked furniture. So we do not need t_{a_print} or t_{a_fold} and set them to zero. For inserting, we can use the value given in Section 7.2.3 for inserting the delivery note with 2.5 s. Additionally, we have to move in order to reach the top of the furniture (MTM-SVL 1.8 s).

$$\begin{aligned} t_{C1\_add\text{-}in} &= (2.5 + 1.8)\ s + 0\ s + 0\ s \\ &= 4.3\ s \end{aligned} \quad (7.14)$$

In order to secure, we mentioned that the unit first is strapped and then stretch wrapped additionally. We already analysed the travel time to reach the central area in Formula 7.11, as well as lifting the unit and putting it down on the stretching machine. The stretching is done mechanically, which can be analysed with 62.3 s (MTM-SVL). Additionally, four straps are necessary and this is done manually, therefore we calculate it with four times 43.2 s (MTM-SVL).

7.4 Case Study

As we have already included the pick-up of the pallet within analysing the transport to the provision area, we do not need to include providing here, and can set $t_{provide}$ to zero.

If we sum up the components of the base time, we end up with

$$\begin{aligned} t_{C1\_base} &= 138.2 \ s + 126.0 \ s + 4.3 \ s + (62.3 + 4 \cdot 43.2) \ s + 0 \ s \\ &= 503.6 \ s \end{aligned} \quad (7.15)$$

Items are usually stacked to pallet height when placing them, and as they are similar or equal there is no need to reposition them. For packing, we need to analyse turns and steps additionally as the items being handled are very large. According to Table 5.3, 4.1 s (MTM-SVL) are necessary for lifting and placing. We add 0.6 s (MTM-SD) for each movement of turning back and forth and stepping back and forth. There was no packing proposal available. Quantity and identity have been checked manually for each item. So we add 1.6 s for the identity check (cf. Section 7.2.4), and for the quantity check the packer ticks off each identified article, which we analyse as 1.4 s. We have to grasp and place the pen as well, so we have to add 2,0 s. This results in

$$\begin{aligned} t_{C1\_item} &= 1 \cdot (4.1 + 2.4) \ s + 0 \ s + 1 \cdot (1.6 + (1.4 + 2.0)) \ s \\ &= 11.5 \ s \end{aligned} \quad (7.16)$$

as item time.

In average there are 36 chairs on a pallet (four times a stack of nine), so in total we have

$$\begin{aligned} t_{C1\_pack} &= t_{travel} + t_{set\text{-}up} + t_{base} + n \cdot t_{item} \\ &= 253.1 \ s + 38.0 \ s + 503.6 \ s + 36 \cdot 11.5 \ s \\ &= 1208.7 \ s \end{aligned} \quad (7.17)$$

where n is the number of articles. In total, we calculated that the packer needs 20 minutes. If we consider the 6 to 15 percent for allowances as well as the 5 to 10 percent for recreation (Dangelmaier 2001, 490), we end up at 25 minutes. The supervisor of this area estimated that a packer needs 26 minutes in average.

This case study illustrated that it is also possible to calculate the cycle time for packing for very specific cases using the formulas determined in Section 6, and that these are not only suitable for the most common cases, but can be applied for specific scenarios as well. This again helped to enhance the credibility of the formulas, especially with regard to the generality and to demonstrate the functionality of the formulas.

To sum up, we successfully validated the structure of the formulas identified in Chapter 6 in this chapter using the two most common cases of packing in distribution centres and enhanced the functional credibility of the formulas by performing a proof of concept for each of the cases and performing a case study on a specific case. This case also helped increasing the credibility in the generality.

8 Conclusion

In this chapter, we summarise the results achieved by this thesis. We also highlight how these can be used in future research, and where there are possibilities to further refine and specify the knowledge gained.

8.1 Summary

In this thesis, we set out to determine cycle times for packing in distribution centres. To achieve this objective, we first took a closer look at distribution centres, packing and cycle time calculations for different systems, as well as their common ground. We also analysed scientific publications, which are related to packing and provide time calculations for the process to emphasise differences between these works and this thesis and highlight approaches which are interesting for our research.

After that, we structured the packing process in distribution centres according to obligatory and optional sub-processes in a process chain. To gain a holistic view, we studied the material flow for which we specified activities included in the sub-processes, as well as the organisation and the information flow. Further, we distinguished the packing process from other packaging activities, resulting in a clearly defined packing process in distribution centres. This structure is already useful in order to identify what needs to be considered, when planning packing areas for distribution centres.

Based on the definition and the process steps, we constructed morphological boxes of parameters influencing the packing time. This resulted in nine morphological boxes, one for each process step. In order to condense them to the most significant parameters, their degree of influence was analysed using analysis of variance (ANOVA). The condensed morphological box includes unit handling, transport, batching, degree of automation and type of the three parameters quality check, protection material and securing method. These most relevant parameters indicate where to start first with improvement efforts. Finally, we summarised implications extracted from this analysis for the derivation of cycle time formulas.

The results of the analysis of variance proved a useful aid to derive the condensed morphological box for all process steps and determine the significance of influencing parameters. Even though the approach is representative and empirical, some issues with the statistical objectivity remain. The first issue is the determination of times for the extreme specifications of the parameters within the analysis of variance. We used the MTM methodology to determine them and tried to standardise specifications, but had to assume a set-up while deriving the required times. Additionally, we used fractional factorial designs for the analysis of variance, which do not consider interactions between parameters. As we wanted to get an idea about their significance and our intention was to solely perform a screening experiment, this still seems to be appropriate. Another problem, which we recognised, is that sometimes the same significance level occurred for parameters, but their share of the total effect differed substantially. This is caused by the upper and lower bounds indicated for the F distribution for the respective significance level. Therefore, we decided to consider both, the significance level and the share, while evaluating the significance of parameters.

Based on the knowledge gained, we determined a basic cycle time calculation for packing in distribution centres and refined its components with more detailed formulas. Due to the chosen detailing level (general applicable for packing in distribution centres), they can only provide a solid basis for further research activities, which should focus on detailing the formulas for different strategies and set-ups.

As the size of the handling unit was identified to be the most significant influencing parameter for almost every process step, we classified packing according to the combination of incoming item size and outgoing shipping unit size. This classification gave the possibility to take a closer look at factors of the cycle time calculation and to validate the design of the general formulas. At the same time, it can be used to compare packing tasks of different distribution centres in a benchmark study. We picked

8.1 Summary

the two most common cases for packing in distribution centres: 'packing articles into packages or small load carriers' and 'packing packages or small load carriers on pallets' to validate the structure of the formulas regarding applicability and generality by refining factors for them. Further, results have been compared with data from distribution centres to enhance the functional credibility of the formulas. Additionally, we used a case study of a very specific packing process to focus on the possibility to generally apply the formulas. All three scenarios proved that the formulas can be applied and used in order to determine cycle times for packing in distribution centres.

In other words, we found formulas, which can be used to plan and optimise packing processes systematically. This takes knowledge on packing one step further: previously, systems needed to be designed by trial and error; in contrast, we are now able to calculate performance. Therefore, oversizing of systems can already be avoided in the design phase of distribution centres and distribution centres can perform more efficiently. We introduced another lever which helps to improve efficiency of existing systems: we identified the time influencing parameters of packing systems and their significance. Improvement work should start considering the most significant parameters first (in summary cf. Table 5.22). Apart from these aspects, we also showed the difference between product packaging and packing in distribution centres as well as how important it is for distribution centres to focus more intensely on this topic in order to improve efficiency. To support improvement work and planning, we structured the packing process according to material and information flow as well as its organisation.

The outcome of this thesis allows calculating the time required for a packing job. Using the determined cycle time formulas in combination with the required amount of packing jobs per day, we can answer the question "How many packing workplaces do I need to be able to handle the required throughput?". Still, for the future, there will be work on refining the results, in the same way as it has been for picking since the 1970ies. We discuss some ideas in the next section.

8.2 Outlook

The determined formulas reflect only the basic structure for calculating cycle times of packing, with some detailed formulas where possible on a general detailing level, as there were no such considerations before. In the future, it is necessary to further specify these general formulas for specific cases, which are related to either the type of certain process steps (like those parameters analysed as very significant in the analysis of variance, cf. Section 5.4), the degree of automation or even to specific strategies which can be used in packing. These strategies need to be developed first.

Also the validation of the general formulas and the specification of factors for further tasks identified in Section 7 can be interesting for further investigations. Additionally, the influence of using average values can be investigated and formulas for other scenarios not using the average, such as best and worst case considerations, can be created. This could serve to validate also the functionality of the formulas.

Another field for further research is to develop standard best-practice workplace layouts for the derived tasks according to influencing parameters. These standard layouts can also optimise workplace set-ups according to the parameters and strategies.

It can also be interesting to include cost analysis to decide on the cost optimal solution. Therefore, it is necessary to specify which technique can be used in which cases and which costs are associated when buying a certain machine, or which other business models could be attractive.

A further avenue for future research is to study the combination of the packing with the picking process, which is usually an upstream process. Interactions between picking and packing can influence the performance of the whole distribution centre significantly. This is particularly true as picking is the most important process in distribution centres regarding costs and working time (WarehouseExcellence-Study 2013) and cycle times already exist for a lot of picking strategies.

Thereafter, also the potential intermediate process of sorting or consolidating should be included into the considerations. Radtke (2000, 133) emphasises that the packing process has an impact on the performance of the sorting system and designates packing a "performance limiting

8.2 Outlook

component" for the sorter. Consequently, investigating on the process combination picking, sorting and packing is a very promising research topic.

Another interesting model, related to the combination of cycle times for picking and packing, can be a cycle time calculation for the so called 'pick and pack' process. Therein, items are directly put into the shipping container and only certain process steps of the packing time determined in this thesis are relevant. Once there are also other possibilities to combine these two processes in calculation models, comparisons for the best implementation can be made according to given requirements.

After considering upstream processes, also downstream steps, for instance the development and combination of cycle times for shipping, are of interest, particularly in order to improve the holistic planning of distribution centres.

Even though there are lots of possibilities for future research, we started highlighting the importance of packing in distribution centres to improve efficiency. We contributed to this purpose by providing formulas to calculate cycle times. This avoids oversizing and helps improve the efficiency of packing processes, which will, in the end, also effect the efficiency of the complete supply-chain as distribution centres are important nodes in these networks.

References

Arnold, D. and K. Furmans (2009, Januar). *Materialfluss in Logistiksystemen* (6 ed.). VDI-Buch. Heidelberg: Springer-Verlag.

Arnold, D., H. Isermann, A. Kuhn, H. Tempelmeier and K. Furmans (2004). *Handbuch Logistik* (2., rev. ed.). Heidelberg: Springer-Verlag.

Arnold, D., H. Isermann, A. Kuhn, H. Tempelmeier and K. Furmans (2008). *Handbuch Logistik* (3., rev. ed.). Heidelberg: Springer-Verlag.

ASTM (1996). Standard Terminology of Packaging and Distribution Environments. Technical report, American Society for Testing and Materials.

ASTM D1974/D1974M - 10 (1974). Standard Practice for Methods of Closing, Sealing, and Reinforcing Fiberboard Boxes. Technical report, American Society for Testing and Materials.

Atz, T. and A. W. Günthner (2011). Integrierte Lagersystemplanung. *Logistics Journal: Proceedings 07*(1), p. 1–21.

Baker, P. (2006). Designing distribution centres for agile supply chains. *International Journal of Logistics: Research & Applications 9*(3), p. 207–221.

Balci, O. (1998). *Handbook of Simulation*, Chapter 10, p. 335–396. New York: John Wiley & Sons.

Bartholdi III, J. J. and S. T. Hackman (2011, August). Warehouse & Distribution Science Release 0.95.

Bleisch, G. (2003). *Lexikon Verpackungstechnik* (1 ed.). Hamburg: Behr's Verlag.

Bleisch, G., J.-P. Majschak and U. Weiß (2011). *Verpackungstechnische Prozesse : Lebensmittel-, Pharma- und Chemieindustrie* (1 ed.). Theorie und Praxis. Hamburg: Behr's Verlag.

Bokranz, R. and K. Landau (2006). *Produktivitätsmanagement von Arbeitssystemen: MTM-Handbuch*. Schäffer-Poeschel Verlag.

Borcherdt, U. (1994, April). *Spielzeitermittlung für Flurförderzeuge zur Regalbedienung mit von der Hubhöhe abhängiger Fahrgeschwindigkeit*. Ph.D. thesis, Universität Stuttgart.

Bowersox, D., D. Closs and M. B. Cooper (2010). *Supply Chain Logistics Management* (3 ed.). McGraw-Hill Education.

Braun, M., S. Koch, J. Böhner, D. Marrenbach and A. Siepenkort (2010). *Der Mensch in der Intralogistik - Ein Handbuch für Führungskräfte*. Universität Stuttgart.

Brody, A. L. and K. S. Marsh (1997). *The Wiley Encyclopeia of packaging Technology*. A Wiley-Interscience publication. John Wiley & Sons, Inc.

Bullinger, H. (1994). *Ergonomie: Produkt- und Arbeitsplatzgestaltung*. Technologiemanagement : wettbewerbsfähige Technologieentwicklung und Arbeitsgestaltung. Teubner B.G. GmbH.

Bundesministerium für Umwelt, Naturschutz und Reaktorsicherheit (2008, April). Verpackungsverordnung - nichtamtliche Lesefasung. http://www.bmu.de. As of April 1st, 2009.

Crostack, H.-A., J. Deuse, C. Goldscheid and N. Schlüter (2007, July). Optimierung von Kommissionierung und Verpackung durch geeignete Strategien für die Qualitätsprüfung unter Berücksichtigung der Retourenabwicklung. Technical report, Dortmunder Initiative zur rechnerintegrierten Fertigung (RIF) e. V.

Crostack, H.-A. and M. ten Hompel (eds.) (2007, October). *Forderungsgerechte Auslegung von intralogistischen Systemen Logistics on Demand*, SFB 696. Praxiswissen Service Verlag.

Dangelmaier, W. (2001). *Fertigungsplanung: Planung von Aufbau und Ablauf der Fertigung*. VDI-Buch. Berlin, Heidelberg: Springer-Verlag.

Dietrich, E. and S. Alfred (2010). *Statistical Procedures for Machine and Process Qualification* (6., rev. ed.). Weinheim, München: Carl Hanser Verlag.

Dietz, G. and R. Lippmann (1986). *Verpackungstechnik*. Wissensspeicher für Technologen. Heidelberg: Hüthig Verlag.

DIN 30781-1 (1989, May). Transport chain; basic concepts. Deutsche Norm, Deutsches Institut für Normung e. V., Berlin.

DIN 55405 (2006, November). Packaging - Terminology - Terms and definitions. Deutsche Norm, Deutsches Institut für Normung e. V., Berlin.

DIN 55479 (2000, March). Packaging - Types of sealings of cartons and boxes by means of pressure-sensitive adhesive tape and gummed paper tape. Deutsche Norm, Deutsches Institut für Normung e. V., Berlin.

DIN 55510-2 (2005, November). Packaging - Dimensional coordination in the field of packaging - Part 2: Terminology. Deutsche Norm, Deutsches Institut für Normung e. V., Berlin.

DIN EN 14053 (2003, September). Packaging - Packagings manufactured from corrugated or solid fibreboard - Types and construction; German version EN 14053:2003. Deutsche Norm, Deutsches Institut für Normung e. V., Berlin.

DIN EN 14943 (2006, March). Transport services - Logistics - Glossary of terms; German version EN 14943:2005. Deutsche Norm, Deutsches Institut für Normung e. V., Berlin.

DIN EN 415-1 (2011, September). Safety of packaging machines - Part 1: Terminology and classification of packing machines and associated equipment; German version prEN 415-1:2011. Deutsche Norm, Deutsches Institut für Normung e. V., Berlin.

Drechsel, D. and F. Vetter (2008). *Wäge-, Abfüll- und Verpackungsprozesse* (2 rev. ed.). München: Oldenbourg Industrieverlag.

Dzeik, V. (2008). *Entwicklung eines Prozesskostenmodells zur Kalkulation von Verpackungskosten manueller Verpackungsarbeitsplätze*. Dissertationsschrift, Wirtschafts- und Sozialwissenschaftliche Fakultät der Technischen Universität Dortmund.

Dzeik, V. and C. Picker (2003). Kalkulation von Verpackungskosten in der Phase der Packmittel- und Produktentwicklung, Schlussbericht zum AiFProjekt Nr. 12834 N. Technical report, Technischen Universität Dortmund.

Ebeling, C. (1990). *Integrated Packaging Systems for Transportation and Distribution*. Packaging and Converting Technology Series. New York: Marcel Dekker INC.

Eschke, R. (2005). *Technische Verpackungslogistik : Auslegung von Verpackungen für den globalen Versand* (2., rev. ed.). Number 379 in Kontakt und Studium. Renningen: expert Verlag.

FEFCO (2007). International fibreboard case code. Technical report, European Federation of Corrugated Board Manufacturers, European Solid Board Organisation.

FEM 9.851 (1978, August). *Serienhebezeuge - Leistungsnachweis für Regalbediengeräte - Spielzeiten.* Technical report, Fédération Européenne de la Manutention.

Fischer, W. and L. Dittrich (2004). *Materialfluß und Logistik: Potentiale vom Konzept bis zur Detailauslegung* (2., ext. ed.). VDI. Berlin: Springer-Verlag.

Frazelle, E. (2002). *Supply Chain Strategy - The Logistics of Supply Chain Management.* McGraw-Hill Companies Inc.

Gassmann, O. and P. Sutter (2008). *Praxiswissen Innovationsmanagement: Von der Idee zum Markterfolg.* München: Carl Hanser Verlag.

Govindaraj, T., E. E. Blanco, D. A. Bodner, M. Goetschalckx, L. F. McGinnis and G. P. Sharp (2000, October). Design of warehousing and distribution systems: an object model offacilities, functions and information. In: *2000 IEEE International Conference on Systems, Man, and Cybernetics*, Volume 2, Nashville, TN, USA, p. 1099–1104.

Großeschallau, W. (1984). *Materialflußrechnung - Modelle und Verfahren zur Analyse und Berechnung von Materialflußsystemen.* Berlin: Springer-Verlag.

Großmann, G. and M. Kaßmann (2007). *Transportsichere Verpackung und Ladungssicherung* (2., rev. ed.). expert Verlag.

Grote, K.-H. (2011). *Dubbel Taschenbuch für den Maschinenbau* (23., rev. and ext. ed.). Berlin: Springer-Verlag.

Gudehus, T. (1973). *Grundlagen der Kommissioniertechnik. Dynamik der Warenverteil- und Lagersysteme.* Essen: W. Girardet.

Gudehus, T. (2006). Masterformeln der Logistik - Teil I Ladeeinheiten, Spielzeiten und Grenzleistungen. *f+h fördern und heben 7-8*, p. 313–315.

Gudehus, T. (2010). *Logistik* (4. ed.), Volume 1: Grundlagen, Verfahren und Strategien. Berlin: Springer-Verlag.

Gudehus, T. (2011). *Logistik : Grundlagen - Strategien - Anwendungen.* Berlin, Heidelberg: Springer-Verlag.

Gudehus, T. and H. Kotzab (2012). *Comprehensive Logistics* (2. ed.). Berlin, Heidelberg: Springer-Verlag.

Günthner, W. A. and U. Lammer (2009). *Funktionsvereinigung in der Lagertechnik - Forschungsbericht.* fml - Lehrstuhl für Fördertechnik Materialfluss Logistik, Technische Universität München.

References

Gustafsson, K., G. Jönson, D. Smith and L. Sparks (2005, July). Packaging logistics and retailers' profitability: an IKEA case study. In: *13th Research Conference of the European Association for Education and Research in Commercial Distribution*.

Harsch, W. and A. Wichmann (1990). *Manuelle Verpackungsarbeitssysteme: Planungsleitfaden*. Number 3 in Manuelle Verpackungsarbeitssysteme. TÜV - Verlag GmbH.

Hartung, J., B. Elpelt and K. Klösener (2009). *Statistik: Lehr- und Handbuch der angewandten Statistik*. München: Oldenbourg Wissenschafts Verlag.

Hauschildt, J. and S. Salomo (2011). *Innovationsmanagement*. Vahlens Handbücher der Wirtschafts- und Sozialwissenschaften. München: Vahlen.

Heinz, K. and R. Olbrich (1989). *Zeitdatenermittlung in indirekten Bereichen*. Schriftenreihe Technische Betriebsführung. Verlag TÜV Rheinland.

Hellström, D. and M. Saghir (2007). Packaging and logistics interactions in retail supply chains. *Packaging Technology and Science 20*(3), p. 197–216.

ISO 7000 (2012). Graphical symbols for use on equipment - Registered symbols. International Standard, International Organization for Standardization, Geneva.

ISO 780 (1997). Packaging - Pictorial marking for handling of goods. International Standard, International Organization for Standardization, Geneva.

Jansen, R. (2008, June). Sicherung von Ladeeinheiten: Wickelstretchen? Aber sicher! *PackReport 6*, p. 58.

Jodin, D. and M. ten Hompel (2006). *Sortier- und Verteilsysteme*. Springer-Verlag, Heidelberg.

John, B. (1987). *Handbuch der Planzeiten-Praxis*. München, Wien: Carl Hanser Fachbuchverlag.

Johnsson, M. (1998). *Packaging Logistics: A Value Added Approach*. Lund University.

Jünemann, R. and T. Schmidt (2000). *Materialflusssysteme* (2. ed.). Heidelberg: Springer-Verlag.

Kleppmann, W. (2011). *Versuchsplanung: Produkte und Prozesse optimieren*. Praxisreihe Qualitätswissen. München: Carl Hanser Fachbuchverlag.

Krottmaier, J. (1994). *Versuchsplanung: Ein integraler Bestandteil der TQM-Strategie* (3., rev. ed.). Praxiswissen für Ingenieure. TÜV Media GmbH TÜV Rheinland Group.

Kuhn, A. (1995). *Prozeßketten in der Logistik, Entwicklungstrends und Umsetzungsstrategien.* Unternehmenslogistik. Dortmund: Verlag Praxiswissen.

Lange, V. (1998). *Integration und Implementierung von Mehrweg-Transport-Verpackungssystemen in bestehende Logistikstrukturen.* Logistik für die Praxis. Dortmund: Verlag Praxiswissen.

Lee, S. G. and S. W. Lye (2003). Design for manual packaging. *International Journal of Physical Distribution & Logistics Management Vol. 33 Iss.*, p. 163–189.

Lindman, H. R. (1992, Februrary). *Analysis of variance in experimental design.* Springer texts in statistics. New York: Springer-Verlag.

Lippolt, C. R. (2003). *Spielzeiten in Hochregallagern mit doppeltiefer Lagerung.* Ph.D. thesis, Universität Karlsruhe (TH), Karlsruhe.

Livingstone, S. and L. Sparks (1994). The New German Packaging Laws: Effects on Firms Exporting to Germany. *International Journal of Physical Distribution & Logistics Management Vol. 24 Iss. 7*, p. 15–25.

Lolling, A. (2003). *Analyse der menschlichen Zuverlässigkeit bei Kommissioniertätigkeiten.* Ph.D. thesis, Fakultät Maschinenbau der Universität Dortmund, Aachen.

Magee, J. F., W. C. Copacino and D. B. Rosenfield (1985, November). *Modern Logistics Management: Integrating Marketing, Manufacturing and Physical Distribution.* Wiley Series on Marketing Management. John Wiley & Sons, Inc.

Martin, H. (2009). *Transport- und Lagerlogistik: Planung, Struktur, Steuerung und Kosten von Systemen der Intralogistik* (7., rev. and ext. ed.). Wiesbaden: Vieweg+Teubner Verlag.

Mayer, S. (2009). Excellence in Logistics - Supply Chain success during the crisis. Technical report, A.T. Kearney.

Maynard, H. B., G. J. Stegemerten and J. L. Schwab (1948). *Methods-time measurement* (1. rev. ed.). New York: McGraw-Hill Book Co.

Meier, M. (2005). Der Innovations-Prozess. Technical report, Eidgenössische Technische Hochschule Zürich.

Menk, J. (1998). *Beitrag zur Planung qualitätsfähiger Kommissioniersysteme - ein humanorientierter Ansatz.* Ph.D. thesis, Universität Dortmund, Fakultät Maschinenbau.

Michel, R., H. D. Torspecken and J. Jandt (2004). *Neuere Formen der Kostenrechnung mit Prozesskostenrechnung.* Kostenrechnung. Carl Hanser Fachbuchverlag.

Montgomery, D. C. (2009). *Design and Analysis of Experiments* (7., international student version ed.). Hoboken, NJ: John Wiley & Sons, Inc.

MTM (2004). Grund- und Standardvorgänge. Datenkarten, Deutsche MTM-Vereinigung e. V.

MTM (2012a). Logistik. Lehrgangsunterlagen, Deutsche MTM-Vereinigung e. V.

MTM (2012b). UAS. Lehrgangsunterlagen, Deutsche MTM-Vereinigung e. V.

Nyhuis, P. and H. P. Wiendahl (2012). *Logistische Kennlinien - Grundlagen, Werkzeuge und Anwendungen* (3 ed.). Berlin Heidelberg: Springer-Verlag, Heidelberg.

Ohno, T. (2009, February). *Das Toyota-Produktionssystem* (2., rev. ed.). Frankfurt am Main: Campus Verag.

Pfohl, H.-C. (2010). *Logistiksysteme: Betriebswirtschaftliche Grundlagen.* Springer-Verlag Berlin Heidelberg.

Pielok, T. (2010). *Prozeßkettenmodulation, Management von Prozeßketten mittels Logistic Function Deployment.* Ph.D. thesis, Fakultät Maschinenbau, Universität Dortmund.

Rabe, M., S. Wenzel and S. Spieckermann (2008). *Verifikation und Validierung für die Simulation in Produktion und Logistik - Vorgehensmodelle und Techniken.* Berlin Heidelberg: Springer-Verlag.

Radtke, A. (2000). *Beitrag zur Entwicklung optimierter Betriebsstrategien für Sortiersysteme.* Logistik für die Praxis. Dortmund: Verlag Praxiswissen.

REFA (1991). *Planung und Steuerung.* Number 3 in Methodenlehre der Betriebsorganisation. Verband für Arbeitsgestaltung, Betriebsorganisation und Unternehmensentwicklung. Carl Hanser Fachbuchverlag.

REFA (1997). *Datenermittlung.* Number 10 in Methodenlehre der Betriebsorganisation. Verband für Arbeitsgestaltung, Betriebsorganisation und Unternehmensentwicklung. Carl Hanser Fachbuchverlag.

Ritchey, T. (2006, March). Problem structuring using computer-aided morphological analysis. *Journal of the Operational Research Society Vol. 57*(7), p. 792–801.

Römisch, P. (2011). *Materialflusstechnik: Auswahl und Berechnung von Elementen und Baugruppen der Fördertechnik.* Wiesbaden: Vieweg+Teubner Verlag.

Rouwenhorst, B., B. Reuter, V. Stockrahm, G. J. an Houtum, R. J. Mantel and W. H. M. Zijm (2000, May). Warehouse design and control: Framework and literature review. *European Journal of Operational Research Vol. 122*(3), p. 515–533.

Rummler, T. and W. Schutt (1991). *Verpackungsverordnung: Praxishandbuch mit Kommentar* (1. ed.). Hamburg: Behr-Verlag.

Sadowsky, V. (2007). *Beitrag zur analytischen Leistungsermittlung von Kommissioniersystemen.* Ph.D. thesis, Universität Dortmund.

Saghir, M. (2004). The concept of packaging logistics. Technical report, Department of Design Sciences, Packaging Logistics, Lund University.

Sarker, B. R. and P. S. Babu (1995, August). Travel time models in automated storage/retrieval systems: A critical review. *International Journal of Production Economics Vol. 40*, p. 173–184.

Sautter, K., E. Westkämper and R. Meyer (eds.) (1998). *Mehr Erfolg durch professionellen Methodeneinsatz. Tagungsband : Eine Empirische Untersuchung zum Methodeneinsatz in Produzierenden Unternehmen. Ergebnisse der Studie. Fachtagung. 18. Juni 1998, Darmstadt.* REFA-Verband für Arbeitsgestaltung, Betriebsorganisation und Unternehmensentwicklung: Fraunhofer IRB Verlag, Stuttgart.

Scherff, U. (1987). Arbeitsplätze in der Verpackung. In: *Verpackungstechnik : Entwicklungen u. Erfahrungen; Tagung, Düsseldorf, 19. Mai 1987*, Number 638 in VDI-Berichte, Düsseldorf. VDI-Verlag.

Schumann, M. (2008). *Zur Bestimmung der Umschlagleistung von Hochregallagern unter besonderer Berücksichtigung der Lagerorganisation.* Ph.D. thesis, Fakultät für Maschinenbau der Technischen Universität Chemnitz.

Schuster, K.-P. (1991). Logistikgerechte Konzeption sowie Realisierung der Produktverpackung und ein praktischer Anwendungsfall. *OR Spektrum 13*, p. 254–263.

Schwab, M., J. Weiblen and K. Furmans (2009, October). Bewertung der Leistungsfähigkeit von Distributionszentren mit dem Kennzahlensystem des "Distribution Center Reference Model" (DCRM). In: *5. Fachkolloquium der Wissenschaftliche Gesellschaft für Technische Logistik (WGTL): Tagungsbeiträge*, p. 311–318. TU Ilmenau Universitätsbibliothek.

Seemüller, S. (2005, October). *Durchsatzberechnung automatischer Kleinteilelager im Umfeld des elektronischen Handels*. Ph.D. thesis, Fakultät für Maschinenwesen, Technische Universität München.

Siebertz, K., D. van Bebber and T. Hochkirchen (2010). *Statistische Versuchsplanung: Design of Experiments (DoE)*. VDI-Buch. Springer-Verlag.

Stock, J. R. (2001). Doctoral Research In Logistics and Logistics-Related Areas: 1992-1998. *Journal of Business Logistics Vol. 22*(1), p. 125–256.

Taguchi, G. (1987). *System of experimental design*. Number 1 in Engineering methods to optimize quality and minimize costs. UNIPUB/Kraus International Publications.

ten Hompel, M. and V. Heidenblut (2011). *Taschenlexikon Logistik - Abkürzungen, Definitionen und Erläuterungen der wichtigsten Begriffe aus Materialfluss und Logistik*. Berlin Heidelberg: Springer-Verlag.

ten Hompel, M. and K. Hömberg (2008). Übersicht analytischer Berechnungsverfahren in Kommissioniersystemen. In: P. Nyhuis (eds.), *Beiträge zu einer Theorie der Logistik*, p. 391–408. Berlin Heidelberg: Springer-Verlag.

ten Hompel, M., V. Sadowsky and M. Beck (2011). *Kommissionierung: Materialflusssysteme 2 - Planung und Berechnung der Kommissionierung in der Logistik*. Materialflusssysteme. Heidelberg Dordrecht London New York: Springer-Verlag.

ten Hompel, M. and T. Schmidt (2010). *Warehouse Management: Organisation und Steuerung von Lager- und Kommissioniersystemen* (4. ed.). Heidelberg: Springer-Verlag.

ten Hompel, M., T. Schmidt and L. Nagel (2007). *Materialflusssysteme: Förder- und Lagertechnik* (3., rev. ed.). Materialflusssysteme. Heidelberg Berlin: Springer-Verlag.

Toutenburg, H., P. Knöfel, I. Kreuzmair, M. Schomaker and D. Williams-Boeker (2009). *Six Sigma: Methoden und Statistik für die Praxis*. Berlin Heidelberg: Springer-Verlag.

Vahrenkamp, R. (2007). *Logistik: Management und Strategien* (6., rev. and ext. ed.). München Wien: Oldenbourg.

VDI 2195 (1985, April). Time and handling rate studies for cranes. VDI Richtlinie, Verein Deutscher Ingenieure, Düsseldorf.

VDI 2516 (2003, September). Floor conveyors for storage and retrieval - Cycle time calculation in narrow aisles. VDI Richtlinie, Verein Deutscher Ingenieure, Düsseldorf.

VDI 3561 (1973, July). Operating test cycles for performance comparison and for the commissioning of stacker-cranes. VDI Richtlinie, Verein Deutscher Ingenieure, Düsseldorf.

VDI 3590-1 (1994, April). Order-picking systems. VDI Richtlinie, Verein Deutscher Ingenieure, Düsseldorf.

VDI 3590-2 (2002, July). Order picking systems - System design. VDI Richtlinie, Verein Deutscher Ingenieure, Düsseldorf.

VDI 3600 (2001, August). Processes and process orientation in production logistics - Example: Automotive Industry. VDI Richtlinie, Verein Deutscher Ingenieure, Düsseldorf.

VDI 3612 (1996, December). Incoming goods / Outgoing goods. VDI Richtlinie, Verein Deutscher Ingenieure, Düsseldorf.

VDI 3633 (1996, November). Simulation of systems in materials handling, logistics and production - Fundamentals. VDI Richtlinie, Verein Deutscher Ingenieure, Düsseldorf.

VDI 3638 (1995, November). Paletising systems. VDI Richtlinie, Verein Deutscher Ingenieure, Düsseldorf.

VDI 3646 (1994, November). Cycletime of continuous transport units in automatic storage systems. VDI Richtlinie, Verein Deutscher Ingenieure, Düsseldorf.

VDI 3968-1 (1994, January). Safety of load units - Specification of demands. VDI Richtlinie, Verein Deutscher Ingenieure, Düsseldorf.

VDI 3968-2 (1994, May). Safety of load units - Organisational and technical methods. VDI Richtlinie, Verein Deutscher Ingenieure, Düsseldorf.

VDI 3968-3 (1994, January). Safety of load units - Strapping systems. VDI Richtlinie, Verein Deutscher Ingenieure, Düsseldorf.

VDI 3968-4 (1994, January). Safety of load units - Shrinking. VDI Richtlinie, Verein Deutscher Ingenieure, Düsseldorf.

VDI 3968-5 (2009, December). Safety of load units - Stretching. VDI Richtlinie, Verein Deutscher Ingenieure, Düsseldorf.

VDI 3978 (1998, August). Achievement and cycle time of piece good conveyor systems. VDI Richtlinie, Verein Deutscher Ingenieure, Düsseldorf.

VDI 4418 (2000, December). Automated storage systems for long and flat-shaped goods. VDI Richtlinie, Verein Deutscher Ingenieure, Düsseldorf.

VDI 4446 (2004, February). Determination of cycle times of cranes. VDI Richtlinie, Verein Deutscher Ingenieure, Düsseldorf.

VDI 4480-2 (2002, July). Throughput of automatic warehouses with non-lane-bound shelf operating systems. VDI Richtlinie, Verein Deutscher Ingenieure, Düsseldorf.

VDI 4490 (2007, May). Operational logistics key figures from goods receiving to dispatch. VDI Richtlinie, Verein Deutscher Ingenieure, Düsseldorf, Düsseldorf.

Verpackungsprojekt (2011). Verbundforschungsprojekt Entwicklung einer Systematik zur Bewertung von Verpackungsbereichen. Unpublished data from research project, Institute for Material Handling and Logistics, Karlsruhe Institute of Technology.

von der Gracht, H. A. (2008). *The Future of Logistics*. Ph.D. thesis, European Business School Oestrich-Winkel.

WarehouseExcellence-Study (2013). A structured and standardized procedure for evaluating the performance of distribution centers. Data from ongoing study, Institute for Material Handling and Logistics, Karlsruhe Institute of Technology.

Weiblen, J. and D. Berbig (2011, October). Milestone presentation for the research project "Entwicklung einer Systematik zur Bewertung von Verpackungsbereichen". Presentation in the context of the 6th Expertworkshop 'Verpackung" of the Intralogistic-Networks in Baden-Württemberg e.V. http://www.intralogistik-bw.de.

Weiblen, J. and D. Berbig (2012, March). Final presentation for the research project "Entwicklung einer Systematik zur Bewertung von Verpackungsbereichen". Presentation in the context of the 7th Expertworkshop 'Verpackung" of the Intralogistic-Networks in Baden-Württemberg e.V. http://www.intralogistik-bw.de.

Weiblen, J., D. Berbig and K. Furmans (2012, July). Development of a systematic method to evaluate packaging areas. In: *25th European Conference on Operational Research*, Vilnius. "Association of

European Operational Research Societies" within the "International Federation of Operational Research Societies" (IFORS).

Weiblen, J. and K. Breiner (2012). Definition of cycle times for packing in distribution centers. In: *Proceedings of the XX. International Conference on Material Handling, Constructions and Logistics (MHCL) 2012*, Belgrade, p. 201–204. Department of Material Handling, Constructions and Logistics, Faculty Of Mechanical Engeering, Belgrade University.

Westkämper, E. (2006). *Einführung in die Organisation der Produktion*. Berlin Heidelberg New-York: Springer-Verlag.

Wiese, D. (1996). *Verpackungstechnik: Mittel und Methoden zur Lösung der Verpackungsaufgabe - Strategien, Entwicklung, Systeme, Packmittel, Maschinen, Prüfung, Kosten*, Chapter Packereiplanung - Packplatzgestaltung, p. 1–20. Heidelberg: Hüthig.

Wisser, J. (2009). *Der Prozess Lagern und Kommissionieren im Rahmen des Distribution Center Reference Model (DCRM)*. Ph.D. thesis, Fakultät für Maschinenbau, Universität Karlsruhe (TH).

Wisser, J. and M. Hinding (2009, May). Aktuelle Erkenntnisse der Warehouse Excellence Studie. Presentation in the context of a meeting of the "Arbeitskreises Fördertechnik, Materialfluss, Logistik (FML) im Bezirksverein Karlsruhe des Vereins Deutscher Ingenieure (VDI)". https://www.vdi.de/ueber-uns/vdi-vor-ort/bezirksvereine/karlsruher-bezirksverein/.

Yam, K. L. (2010). *The Wiley Encyclopedia of Packaging Technology* (3. ed.). Hoboken, NJ: John Wiley & Sons, Inc.

Zwicky, F. (1966). *Entdecken, Erfinden, Forschen im morphologischen Weltbild*. München Zürich: Droemersche Verlagsanstalt Th. Knaur Nachf.

A Detailed Analysis of Set-up Times for P10

Specified job			6.7 s
Comparing order code with order (3 trials)	SVL	IAVW	4.9 s
Movement between orders	SVL	KA	1.8 s
Priority			**2.5 s**
Comparing priority signs	SVL	IAVE	1.1 s
Changing of eye focus	SVL	GBV	1.4 s
Pick randomly			**1.8 s**
Searching next job	SVL	IAVE	1.1 s
Changing of eye focus	SVL	GBV	0.7 s

Table A.1: Detailed analysis of 'choosing job' (P10)

Manual			3.4 s
Signing paper once	SVL	IAKK	1.4 s
Putting signal	SVL	HUKA	2.0 s
Manual input			**3.2 s**
Input of code into computer	SVL	IDTW	2.3 s
Confirmation of input	SVL	IDTE	0.9 s
Manual/automated			**2.2 s**
Scanning code	SVL	IDES	2.2 s

Table A.2: Detailed analysis of 'confirmation on start' (P10)

Manual comparison			**2.3 s**
Comparing order code with order once	SVL	IAVW	1.6 s
Changing of eye focus	SVL	GBV	0.7 s
Manual/automated			**2.2 s**
Scanning of order	SVL	IDES	2.2 s

Table A.3: Detailed analysis of 'identification' (P10)

Packer's decision			**6.5 s**
Identify four characteristics (e.g. weight, size, transport distance and number of articles) and compare it with packaging alternatives	SVL	IAVW	6.5 s
Standard			**2.2 s**
Compare two characteristics with standard	SVL	IAVE	2.2 s
Provided proposal			**0.9 s**
Read proposal	SVL	IALW	0.9 s

Table A.4: Detailed analysis of 'decision on packaging' (P10)

Packer's decision			6.5 s
Identify sensitivity and weight of four articles	SVL	IAVW	6.5 s
Standard			**2.2 s**
Compare two characteristics with standard	SVL	IAVE	2.2 s
Provided proposal			**0.9 s**
Read proposal	SVL	IALW	0.9 s

Table A.5: Detailed analysis of 'decision on protection material' (P10)

Packer's decision			6.5 s
Identify four characteristics (e.g. size, packing scheme, transport distance and sensitivity of articles) and compare it with securing alternatives	SVL	IAVW	6.5 s
Standard			**2.2 s**
Compare two characteristics with standard	SVL	IAVE	2.2 s
Provided proposal			**0.9 s**
Read proposal	SVL	IALW	0.9 s

Table A.6: Detailed analysis of 'decision on securing method' (P10)

Manual input			3.2 s
Input of code into computer	SVL	IDTW	2.3 s
Confirmation of input	SVL	IDTE	0.9 s
Manual/automated			**2.2 s**
Scanning code	SVL	IDES	2.2 s

Table A.7: Detailed analysis of 'initialisation print' (P10)

Signing			**19.6 s**
Taking pencil	SVL	EH	2.0 s
Writing address (7 words)	SVL	IAKW	17.6 s
Glueing			**6.8 s**
Taking glue	SVL	EH	2.0 s
Taking label and attach it	UAS	ZC3	2.0 s
Glueing	UAS	M-BQB	2.9 s
Self adhesive			**2.3 s**
Taking label and attach it	SVL	IAEU	2.3 s

Table A.8: Detailed analysis of 'marking' (P10)

B Detailed Analysis of Set-up Times for P5

Specified job			8.5 s
Comparing order code with order (3 trials)	SVL	IAVW	4.9 s
Movement between orders	SVL	KA	3.6 s
Priority			**4.0 s**
Comparing priority signs	SVL	IAVE	1.1 s
Changing of eye focus	SVL	GBV	2.9 s
Pick randomly			**2.5 s**
Searching next job	SVL	IAVE	1.1 s
Changing of eye focus	SVL	GBV	1.4 s

Table B.1: Detailed analysis of 'choosing job' (P5)

Manual			**4.3 s**
Signing paper once	SVL	IAKK	1.4 s
Putting signal	SVL	HUKA	2.0 s
Movement to put signal	SVL	KA	0.9 s
Manual input			**4.1 s**
Input of code into computer	SVL	IDTW	2.3 s
Confirmation of input	SVL	IDTE	0.9 s
Movement to reach computer	SVL	KA	0.9 s
Manual/automated			**3.1 s**
Scanning code	SVL	IDES	2.2 s
Movement to reach computer	SVL	KA	0.9 s

Table B.2: Detailed analysis of 'confirmation on start' (P5)

Manual comparison			**3.1 s**
Comparing order code with order once	SVL	IAVW	1.6 s
Changing of eye focus	SVL	GBV	1.4 s
Manual/automated			**3.1 s**
Scanning of order	SVL	IDES	2.2 s
Movement to reach computer	SVL	KA	0.9 s

Table B.3: Detailed analysis of 'identification' (P5)

Packer's decision			3.2 s
Identify two characteristics (e.g. size and number of articles) and compare it with packaging alternatives	SVL	IAVW	3.2 s
Standard			**1.1 s**
Compare one characteristic with standard	SVL	IAVE	1.1 s
Provided proposal			**0.9 s**
Read proposal	SVL	IALW	0.9 s

Table B.4: Detailed analysis of 'decision on packaging' (P5)

Packer's decision			5.4 s
Identify sensitivity of four articles	SVL	IAVW	5.4 s
Standard			**1.1 s**
Compare characteristic with standard	SVL	IAVE	1.1 s
Provided proposal			**0.9 s**
Read proposal	SVL	IALW	0.9 s

Table B.5: Detailed analysis of 'decision on protection material' (P5)

Packer's decision			6.5 s
Identify four characteristics (e.g. size, packing scheme, transport distance and sensitivity of articles) and compare it with securing alternatives	SVL	IAVW	6.5 s
Standard			**2.2 s**
Compare two characteristics with standard	SVL	IAVE	2.2 s
Provided proposal			**0.9 s**
Read proposal	SVL	IALW	0.9 s

Table B.6: Detailed analysis of 'decision on securing method' (P5)

Manual input			**4.1 s**
Input of code into computer	SVL	IDTW	2.3 s
Confirmation of input	SVL	IDTE	0.9 s
Movement to reach computer	SVL	KA	0.9 s
Manual/automated			**3.1 s**
Scanning code	SVL	IDES	2.2 s
Movement to scam	SVL	KA	0.9 s

Table B.7: Detailed analysis of 'initialisation print' (P5)

Signing			**20.5 s**
Taking pencil	SVL	EH	2.0 s
Writing address (7 words)	SVL	IAKW	17.6 s
Movement to write	SVL	KA	0.9 s
Glueing			**7.7 s**
Taking glue	SVL	EH	2.0 s
Taking label and attach it	UAS	ZC3	2.0 s
Glueing	UAS	M-BQB	2.9 s
Movement to glue	SVL	KA	0.9 s
Self adhesive			**3.2 s**
Taking label and attach it	SVL	IAEU	2.3 s
Movement to label	SVL	KA	0.9 s

Table B.8: Detailed analysis of 'marking' (P5)

C Glossary of Notations

C.1 Notations Chapter 3.3

Index	Description
t_{cycle}	Cycle time
$t_{variable}$	Time shares of cycle times with a variable duration
$t_{constant}$	Time shares of cycle times with a constant duration
$\mu_{P1,T}$	Packing performance
$m_{P1,T}$	Number of items that need to be packed in one sorting batch by one packer
T_{BT}	Process time for one packer
$T_{P1,Wait}$	Unproductive times
$T_{Pack,Item\ i}$	Time to pick item i of the sorting batch and pack it into shipping container or on pallet
$m_{P1,A}$	Number of orders of a sorting batch which have to be packed by one packer
$T_{Travel,ES\ j}$	Travel time for distance to destination j of the sorter
$T_{Base,ES\ j}$	Preparing work at destination j of the sorter and
$T_{Finish,ES\ j}$	Finishing work at destination j of the sorter
v_{walk}	Velocity of the packer
a_b	Acceleration/deceleration of the packer

$\bar{l}_{(j)}$	Mean distance to destination j
d	Distance between two neighbouring destinations
n	Number of destinations served by one packer
i	A destination of the sorter
j	The neighbouring destination of the sorter

C.2 Notations Chapter 5.3

p	Number of independent generators in fractional factorial designs
k	Number of parameters in fractional factorial designs
N	Number of runs in DOE
a	Number of parameter levels
df_X	Degrees of freedom of one parameter
df_T	Total degrees of freedom of experiment
df_E	Degrees of freedom of the error
SS_T	Corrected sum of squares
n	Number of observations
y_{ij}	ijth observation
$\bar{y}_{..}$	Grand average of all the observations
$\bar{y}_{i.}$	Average of the observations under the ith treatment
$SS_{Treatments}$	Differences between treatment averages
SS_E	Differences within treatment averages due to random errors
$\tau_.$	Treatment mean
F_0	Ratio between differences between and within treatment averages
$MS_{Treatments}$	Mean square of differences between treatment averages
MS_E	Mean square of differences within treatment averages
α	Level of significance
$p_{Treatment}$	Percentage that can be accounted for by the variation of the levels of the respective parameter

C.3 Notations Chapter 6 and 7

$t_{packing}$	Total time for packing
t_{var}	Time shares of the packing time with a variable duration
t_{const}	Time shares of the packing time with a constant duration
t_{travel}	Travel time
t_{set-up}	Set-up time
t_{base}	Base time
t_{item}	Item time
n	Number of articles per outgoing packing unit
t_{t_supply}	Time required to reach a supply area and return
$t_{t\_provide}$	Time required to reach a provision area and return
f_o	Supply consolidation factor
f_p	Provision consolidation factor
$t_{t\_central}$	Time required to reach a central area and return
f_c	Consolidation factor for transport to central area
t_{t_x}	Individual travel time for the respective activity x
v	Maximum velocity
b	De-/acceleration constant
d	Travel distance
t_{pick}	Time to pick up the unit or device
t_{place}	Time to place the unit or device
t_{choose}	Time required for choosing the job
$t_{confirm}$	Time required to confirm the start
$t_{identify}$	Time required to identify the job
$t_{d\_packaging}$	Time required to decide on packaging material
$t_{d\_protect}$	Time required to decide on protection material
t_{d_secure}	Time required to decide on securing material
t_{print}	Time required to initialize printing
t_{mark}	Time required for marking the unit
$t_{prepare}$	Time required to prepare the packaging

$t_{protect}$	Time required for protecting
t_{add-in}	Time required to insert add-ins
t_{secure}	Time required for securing
$t_{provide}$	Time required for providing
t_{p_set-up}	Time required to set-up the packaging
$t_{p\_fixjoint}$	Time required to fix the joints
$t_{p\_assemble}$	Time required to assemble a loading unit
$t_{p\_position}$	Time required to position a loading unit
t_{p_open}	Time required to open a loading unit
t_{a_insert}	Time required to insert an add-in into a messenger bag
t_{a_print}	Time required to print an add-in
t_{a_fold}	Time required to fold an add-in
f_r	Repositioning factor
t_{pack}	Time required to picking up the items and placing them
$t_{proposal}$	Time required to study the packing proposal
f_s	Sample size factor for checking
t_{check}	Time required for checking